STUDIES IN
ANTHROPOLOGICAL METHOD

General Editors

GEORGE AND LOUISE SPINDLER

Stanford University

THE STUDY OF
LITERATE CIVILIZATIONS

THE STUDY OF LITERATE CIVILIZATIONS

FRANCIS L. K. HSU

Northwestern University

HOLT, RINEHART AND WINSTON
New York   Chicago   San Francisco   Atlanta
Dallas   Montreal   Toronto   London   Sydney

FOREWORD

ABOUT THE SERIES

Anthropology has been, since the turn of the century, a significant influence shaping Western thought. It has brought into proper perspective the position of our culture as one of many and has challenged universalistic and absolutistic assumptions and beliefs about the proper condition of man. Anthropology has been able to make this contribution mainly through its descriptive analyses of non-Western ways of life. Only in the last decades of its comparatively short existence as a science have anthropologists developed systematic theories about human behavior in its transcultural dimensions, and only very recently have anthropological techniques of data collection and analysis become explicit and in some instances replicable.

Teachers of anthropology have been handicapped by the lack of clear, authoritative statements of how anthropologists collect and analyze relevant data. The results of fieldwork are available in the ethnographies and they can be used to demonstrate cultural diversity and integration, social control, religious behavior, marriage customs, and the like, but clear, systematic statements about how the facts are gathered and interpreted are rare in the literature readily available to students. Without this information the alert reader of anthropological literature is left uninformed about the process of our science, knowing only the results. This is an unsatisfying state of affairs for both the student and the instructor.

This series is designed to help solve this problem. Each study in the series focuses upon manageable dimensions of modern anthropological methodology. Each one demonstrates significant aspects of the processes of gathering, ordering, and interpreting data. Some are highly selected dimensions of methodology. Others are concerned with the whole range of experience involved in studying a total society. These studies are written by professional anthropologists who have done fieldwork and have made significant contributions to the science of man and his works. In them the authors explain how they go about this work, and to what end. We think they will be helpful to students who want to know what processes of inquiry and ordering stand behind the formal, published results of anthropology.

ABOUT THE AUTHOR

Francis L. K. Hsu received his B.A. in sociology from the University of Shanghai in 1933 and his Ph.D. in anthropology from the University of London in 1941. He taught anthropology at National Yunnan University from 1941–1944, at Columbia University from 1944–1945, and at Cornell University from 1945–1947. He joined the faculty of Northwestern University in 1947, where he is now professor of anthropology and chairman of the Department of Anthropology. He has carried out fieldwork in Southwestern China, India, and Japan and has traveled and lectured extensively throughout the United States and the Far East. His main interests are: comparative studies of literate civilizations, such as China, India, Japan, and the United States; psychological anthropology, especially as it bears on the interlinkage between different aspects of each culture; and kinship (the elementary social grouping in which nearly every human being is raised) as a microcosm linking the individual with the patterns of behavior and culture of his society as a whole. He is the author of a number of books, including *Under the Ancestors' Shadow* (1948; revised edition, 1967), *Americans and Chinese: Two Ways of Life* (1955; revised edition, 1968), and *Clan, Caste and Club* (1963).

ABOUT THE BOOK

Studies of literate civilizations have not been a part of the main stream of anthropological literature. In a rapidly modernizing world, the need for such studies is apparent. This book is an attempt to provide working models, with appropriate illustrations, for the study of literate civilizations. Less than one-third of the book is, however, devoted to the models themselves, since the author has a broader purpose. He assesses the present anthropological concern with the study of literate civilizations—its problems and its proper place in our discipline.

In the first section the author critiques various types of works on literate civilizations, ranging through those which deal with some single aspect of a society, others which deal with generalizable personality characteristics, some of which are confined to life in a single village or community, and those which attempt to understand the underlying unitary characteristics of a society (often labeled "national character studies").

The remainder of the book is devoted to a discussion of problems encountered in the study of literate civilizations and an explication of two approaches which may serve as models. Dr. Hsu discusses the difficult problem of dealing with class, caste, and regional differences, pointing to the importance of identifying the unifying features of a civilization even though recognizing the differences. Another difficulty discussed by the authors, which workers in this area of study face, is the sampling problem. He points out that the matter of coverage is strictly relative. Students of literate societies often have the advantage in that they have records and reports on which to rely.

Under the heading "Some Guiding Principles" Dr. Hsu considers the matter of providing social and cultural context for the village study. He states that we may, in this case, ignore time differences existing between the written materials and the contemporary sociological facts collected at present and concentrate on the *relationships* between the structural patterns in the two kinds of data. In this same section Dr. Hsu discusses the merits of the comparative approach for the study of literate civilizations. He contrasts the comparative approach with the cross-cultural approach and also distinguishes between the pseudocomparative approach and the controlled comparison.

The final resolution of the problem discussed is in the form of models for the study of literate civilizations. They consist of (1) the postulates of a society (ethnographically derived) used as a basis for comparison and contrast, and (2) kinship used as a base for comparisons of societies. The two models are interrelated, since kinship patterns suggest "the basic mechanism through which each society manufactures the appropriate psychological responses vis-à-vis its over-all postulates in its new members from generation to generation."

The book contains a useful bibliography of studies of literate civilizations and communities within them, plus some annotated references offered as an aid to students.

Guidelines are needed as an aid in the training of future anthropologists, most of whom will be working in literate or rapidly modernizing areas of the world. This volume provides a timely orientation to this type of study. Hopefully, it will stimulate others to develop methods and concepts appropriate to the changing environment and objectives of anthropological research.

GEORGE AND LOUISE SPINDLER
General Editors
Phlox, Wisconsin, October 1968

ACKNOWLEDGMENTS

In the preparation of this book I am indebted to Ethel Albert, Paul J. Bohannan, Ronald Cohen, E. Adamson Hoebel, Robert Hunt, Lewis Langness, Thomas P. Rohlen, and George and Louise Spindler for constructive criticisms. Needless to say, I alone am responsible for the opinions and conclusions. I am also very grateful to Mrs. Andrea Sherwin and Mrs. Adele Andelson, whose unfailing research and secretarial help have made this work possible. I am also indebted to Northwestern University's Council of Intersocietal Studies for a grant-in-aid which facilitated the research and preparation of the manuscript for publication.

F. L. K. H.

CONTENTS

1

Introduction

Though generally known as students of primitive society, all anthropologists have, in one way or another, a great deal to do with literate civilizations. They live most of their lives in them; their discipline is part of at least one such civilization; and an increasing number are actually making formal studies of them. Nevertheless, the question of the place of the study of literate civilizations in anthropology is still widely debated.

This book assumes such studies to be not only legitimate but actually necessary if anthropology is to advance and continue to be relevant to the study of man. I will attempt here to assess in its present state the anthropological concern with the study of literate civilizations, its problems, and its proper place in our discipline. I shall also discuss the achievements, theoretical perspectives, and methodological procedures, some of which may make future endeavors more intellectually fruitful for the science of man as a whole.

To begin, by literate I mean just what most people mean—the ability to write a spoken language. I assume that when enough people in a given society have this ability so that a literature is developed, the society can be called literate. Today in our shrinking world there are very few societies which are not literate or rapidly becoming so according to my definition. In the last few decades, for example, there has been a wonderful outpouring of literature from Africa, a continent until recently regarded as nonliterate. I have chosen to use the word civilization because, in contrast to society or culture, it implies an extra increment of scope and elaboration. In this regard the literate civilizations of the world are those which have been literate long enough to have accumulated a wealth of written documents of all sorts and a set of rich intellectual traditions—religious, historical, legal, scientific, and the like. While perhaps all societies are self-conscious, only the literate civilizations have recorded the history of their internal discussions of the questions which absorb them. Ancient Egypt, Rome, and Greece, China, India, Islam, Europe, and the United States of America are examples of literate civilizations, while the societies of the Pacific islands, of most of Africa, and the American Indians are not, though many of them are rapidly developing literate traditions.

What, one might ask, distinguish the studies of India or the United States made by anthropologists from studies by members of other disciplines? Undoubtedly in some cases there are no differences; however, on the whole, anthropologists take with them to the study of any society certain peculiar attitudes. They generally spend an extended period living with the people they study (participant observation), whereas members of other disciplines are much more oriented toward library, statistical material, or questionnaire kinds of approach. In terms of theory, anthropologists are more interested in clarifying the integral nature of diverse aspects of social life and less likely to be narrowly specialized than scholars in other fields. Thirdly, anthropologists concern themselves primarily with factors which are revealed by cross-cultural studies—those which are most significant in explaining intercultural differences, rather than in those factors which serve only to distinguish intracultural variations. These differences between the anthropologist and the sociologist may be illustrated by their respective approaches to divorce in, say, the United States. The sociologist would probably explain our divorce rate in terms of its correlation with incompatability—religious, educational, sexual, or other—between spouses, or with economic prosperity or war conditions; the anthropologist would consider the same phenomenon in the context of different ideologies and institutional patterns among many whole societies. The sociologist with his single society sample might quite successfully predict the rhythm of divorce under conditions which he assumes to be constant within our society, such as the meaning of marriage. However, the anthropologist, with his cross-cultural sample and his concern for the different "givens" assumed by each society (for example, marriage is based initially on love in the United States, but not in Japan), is in a better position to explain why our divorce rate is high or low in comparison with others. Both approaches are certainly valid and are, in fact, complementary. I suggest that the reader keep these distinctions in mind while he follows what I have to say in the rest of the book.

Anthropology as a discipline began in the middle of the nineteenth century. During its first half century, the questions it faced dealt for the most part with theories of social and cultural evolution. Anthropology's domain was specifically those societies, archaic or existent, which were said to represent the stages of human existence that preceded civilization (particularly Western civilization). The interest in European life by early anthropologists was restricted to what they regarded as the cultural debris of much earlier periods of European history— such as myths, superstitions, and children's games. At the same time that anthropologists were seeking the "primitive," a tremendous expansion of Western contact with the non-Western world stimulated the study of non-Western literate civilizations (such as India, China, Indonesia, and Japan) by missionaries, traders, colonial officers, and an occasional traveling scholar. Their investigations were admirably thorough and remain even today quite influential. The empirical groundwork for the study of literate civilizations was thus begun not by formally trained social scientists, but rather by enthusiastic amateurs who might have read some anthropology, but who were certainly not anthropologists.

By the second decade of this century things started to change. Men like Edward Sapir began to suggest that anthropology had something to say, not only about "primitive" life but about civilized society as well (Sapir 1924, 1927). A sociology professor in a missionary university in China, Daniel H. Kulp, produced what appears to be the first community study in a literate civilization (1925). Concurrently, community studies, influenced by anthropological research methods, began to find a place in American sociology. Robert and Helen Lynd's classic study of Middletown in the late 1920s was followed by the works of Lloyd Warner and associates, which led, on much later dates, to his well-known Yankee City series (and other books). Robert Redfield's study of a Mexican village (1930) must be regarded as the first anthropological effort to deal with a literate civilization. Later he was to be the chief architect of a theory of peasant communities and leading sponsor of community studies in literate civilizations.

The now very famous works of Margaret Mead, Ruth Benedict, and James West began in the 1930s as they combined (some with the cooperation of Linton and Kardiner) psychological insights with anthropological perspectives. West's study was of a local American community in the mid-West. Mead's and Benedict's writings illuminated problems in contemporary American culture by analyzing forces at work among nonliterate ways of life. However, although anthropological interest in literate civilizations has grown since then, most anthropologists have remained shy of full-scale treatment of American life.

There are a few important points we should note about the history of the study of literate civilizations. When anthropologists finally turned to literate civilizations, their research usually assumed one of three forms: (1) investigation of a single aspect of a literate civilization, (2) investigation of a single community within a literate civilization, or (3) a broadly psychological approach to the literate civilization as a whole.

The first group concerned itself with religion, politics, art and literature, economics, and the like. Often this kind of study by anthropologists is not distinguishable from those by practitioners of other social sciences and the humanities, especially when the latter work on societies other than their own, and have adopted the anthropologist's interest in cultural factors. The second group chose to turn away from the often voluminous traditional literature and dealt with what the people of the local community said and did. They attempted to explicate how the basic elements of the civilization are integrated in the small community. Even though the villagers studied may be illiterate, the effects of the literate tradition are, nonetheless, in part observable.

The third group emphasized the shared patterns between the written literature, novels, movies, folktales, the sacred books, traditional philosophies, and such, and the values, feelings, and preoccupations of the common people as expressed through their activities, problems, and utterances. Since these anthropologists are most often psychologically oriented, they attempt to assess common psychological patterns which underlie and unite the disparate aspects of each civilization. They look for personality traits, value orientations, or rules of conduct shared by a majority of the people. They try to draw over-all and comprehensive (sometimes considered sweeping) generalizations on the characteristics of larger societal wholes, and are known as national character studies.

For a long time past, and still to a great extent today, the latter two kinds of investigations are closely allied with the anthropological approach to literate civilizations. Obviously the existence of a great body of traditional literature complicates the problem of making conclusions about such societies. The variations and contradictions involved emerge with greater clarity when a wealth of details are present. Anthropologists, accustomed to dealing with little-studied cultures about which they could make facile conclusions, were forced, when they began to work in literate civilizations, to develop new strategies to deal with such complications. The second and third approaches may be regarded as anthropological responses to such complications.

It is interesting to note that, as our discipline progresses, the first approach has also gained momentum in anthropology. This is related in part to the fact that as more economists, historians, political scientists, psychologists, and others have begun to work abroad, they have today adopted much of the anthropologists' interest in cultural factors.

In thinking about the various anthropological approaches to literate civilizations and to facilitate the reading of the rest of this book, it is suggested that the reader consider the simple diagram below:

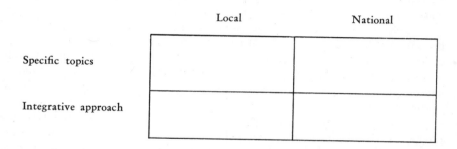

	Local	National
Specific topics		
Integrative approach		

A study, for example, of Japanese literature would be national in scope, but specific to one aspect of Japanese civilization, while one of a Japanese village market would be both specific and local. A study of an Indian village and the national character of Germany are both integrative in intent, but one of the latter is broader than the former in scope. Obviously, as we move from the specific and local to the integrative and national the amount of relevant information increases, the variety of required data changes, and the ground each generalization is designed to cover expands. A few examples from each category will be discussed in the first three chapters of the book. Since the major part of my career has been spent attempting the third or national character type of investigation, I will have more to say about it than about the other approaches. I shall devote the remainder of the book to a discussion of several problems in the study of each literate civilization as a whole and explicate two kinds of inquiry which promise to improve it.

Three major problems are dealt with in Chapter 7, two having to do with the size and complexity of most literate civilizations: class, caste, and regional differences and the sampling problem. The third involves what seems to be a reluctance on the part of many anthropologists to study their own cultures. The latter is a shackle which has vitiated our understanding of many widespread phenomena such as witch hunting, religious persecution, and culture change. Chapter 7 provides the reader with some guiding principles for the study of literate civilizations. How does one delineate the total culture of each complex society? How does one contextualize the small village community in terms of its wider cultural milieu? Why do we need the comparative approach, and what makes for scientifically acceptable comparisons?

In the next two chapters (8 and 9) I set forth two lines along which the study of literate civilizations will become most fruitful: (1) through the use of the concept of postulates as developed by Hoebel (1954) we shall be able to ascertain most or all of the important points of reference of a literate civilization, especially if we make general use of the comparative approach (Chapter 8); (2) by concentrating on a new way of looking at kinship we may have found a key to the interconnections among diverse aspects of a civilization, ranging from its definition of maturity to its house and habitation patterns (Chapter 9).

Both lines of inquiry proposed here have their roots in the traditional anthropological concern with nonliterate societies. The first, Hoebel's, developed out of his study of law among Eskimo, Ifugao, American Indians such as the Cheyenne, the Trobriand Islanders, and the Ashanti. The second, the study of kinship, has been such a sustained and central part of traditional anthropology that to point out its connection with our work on nonliterate societies is sheer redundance. As the reader will find in the following pages, both can be used to form an effective bridge between the study of nonliterate and literate civilizations.

This is not a manual of field techniques. [For that purpose the reader should consult works such as Beardsley's *Field Guide to Japan* (1959).] Although intended for undergraduate students in anthropology, this statement of new lines of inquiry and methodological considerations may nevertheless be of interest to more advanced scholars.

2

The Microscopic and the Wholistic

THE ANTHROPOLOGICAL TRADITION has always centered on the out-of-the way and especially small societies of the world. At first the rationale for this concentration was the discoverey of early stages of cultural evolution. When this rationale became less and less tenable, anthropologists continued studies in these societies explaining that because they are small and relatively simple they allow the fieldworker to approach them microscopically and yet see the whole.

I remember visiting with Melford Spiro in 1948 when he had just returned from Ifaluk, a South Seas atoll with a population of about 240. He displayed in his small living room less than fifty items, including utensils and coconut-fiber mats. He assured me that I was looking at the Ifaluk material culture in its entirety. I also remember a conversation with Herskovits in which he told me that he had everything that was ever written about the Dahomey. Spiro was not being facetious, and Herskovits was not given to exaggeration. Although Herskovits could not duplicate Spiro's feat by displaying all Dahomey material culture in one small living room (since the technology of Dahomey is much more complex than that of Ifaluk), he and Spiro dealt either with an extremely small society or a society without a written history. They could be quite confident about "complete" coverage.

Not always, however, have the "tribes" studied been as small and homogeneous as their students would imply. Contrast, for example, the following societies, all treated in generally the same manner by our profession: Yoruba (4 million), Ibo (4–8 million), Ruanda (2 million), Tikopia (1400), Alor (600), and Kaska Indians (175).[1]

It is probably true that the "communities" actually studied by all anthropologists in all tribes are about the same size, say, roughly 600 people or less.

---

[1] There are large discrepancies in the population estimates for various African tribes. For example, Murdock (1959) estimates the Yoruba at 1,600,000 and the Ibo at 1,000,000, but more recent estimates for these and other groups are generally much higher.

Intensive contact with more people during less than two years (and most field jobs even yet are not much over one) is simply not physically possible. However, the results from the similar-sized samples are assumed to be equally applicable to both the larger social and cultural universes and the smaller.

We simply do not have satisfactory methodological distinctions which would enable us to see now the cultural relationship between, say, the 600 people of an Ibo community and the large population of Ibo is different from that between the same-sized group and the much smaller population of Tikopia.

Even though the methodological difficulties in dealing with large, nonliterate societies are considerable, they are dwarfed by those confronting students of most literate societies. These enormous, literate, and historical societies have each been studied and written about by native and foreign specialists in diverse fields for many generations, and the anthropologist is at once confronted with mountains of material, the study of a small part of which tends to be a lifetime work.[2]

It is true, of course, as Friedl pointed out (1962), that students of old national cultures enjoy certain advantages. Here the anthropologist "need not act as his own historian, economist, political scientist," and the like, but "can consult the works of other specialists." Nor does he "have to discover the structure of the language for himself," or limit his vocabulary "to what he can learn directly from the people he studies" (Friedl 1962: 4–5). However, there is not only the problem of quantitative coverage but also the difficulty of agreement among different specialists, on the one hand, in considering the same aspect of a culture and, on the other hand, in considering the interrelationships between different aspects of that culture.[3]

An example will illustrate some of these difficulties. The caste system of India has been a subject of much writing, from Sanskrit scholars, English colonial officials, and Indian philosophers to modern and non-Indian sociologists and anthropologists. However, to date we still find no agreement on the number of castes (or subcastes), or the criteria for caste ranking, not to mention such wider problems as caste evolution and the significance of caste for social and cultural development.

The anthropologist's difficulties are even more compounded when he tries to make some scientific statements about the culture or cultures of the United States. For one thing he is so unconsciously involved in it that he may be unwilling or unable to see the culture with any except certain biased perceptions that accord with his upbringing. For another, he is likely to meet with objections from individuals whose direct experiences do not agree with his findings, from special interest groups which regard them as offensive, and from academicians who have long marked out certain areas for their private preserves and resent his intrusion.

Yet the inclusion of large, literate societies within the total arena of

---

[2] To some extent this is already true of societies such as that of the Kanuri of Bornu (Cohen 1967), which Cohen calls a semiliterate society since a great deal of their history is recorded.

[3] Consider, for example, the fact that there are approximately 500 specialists on south Asia (India, Pakistan, and Ceylon) in the Association of Asian Studies.

study for the anthropologist is imperative. There is no scientific justification for confining ourselves to one arbitrarily defined kind of society. Physical anthropologists deal with the physical characteristics of all branches of mankind, just as linguists deal with all types of languages. This is, of course, as it should be. Zoology cannot confine its deliberations to horses and cows or lizards and fish. Any science of society and culture must be based on the data found in all types of human societies, wherever they occur. We face a dilemma. We need to cover all forms of society and culture for a sound science of man, but our microscopic methods and desire for integration come into direct opposition one to the other when we undertake the study of literate civilizations.

3

Studies of Specific Topics

ANY ANTHROPOLOGISTS have sought to answer a set of questions about the nature of some specific aspect of a literate civilization. The variety of topics is considerable. For example, besides the community and national character studies, the following topics are a fair but brief sample of the books and articles on Japan: the history of landowning patterns and village social structure, customs relating to household ancestor shrines, labor immigration and industrialization, inheritance and descent, factory management, achievement motivation, language use and the social class of speaker and addressee, Zen Buddhism, patient-nurse relations in a psychiatric hospital, the organization of flower-arranging schools, and interpersonal relations among gangsters. A complete list of the subjects engaging anthropological attention in literate civilizations would, however, cover most of the questions they are asking elsewhere, with the obvious exception of problems specifically related to nomads, hunting and gathering societies, and the like. On the other hand, many studies of specific aspects of literate civilizations by nonanthropologists are not always different from work anthropologists have done in Africa and elsewhere. For example, Takahito Iwai's *The Outline of Tenrikyo* (1932), William A. Aston's *Shinto, the Way of the Gods* (1905), and Serge Elisseeff's *The Mythology of Japan* (1963) combined are comparable in scope to Herskovits and Herskovits *An Outline of Dahomean Religious Beliefs* (1933). William Hugh Erskine's book on *Japanese Festival and Calendar Lore* (1933) and Wolfram Eberhard's *Chinese Festivals* (1952) are similar to George Eaton Simpson's work on *The Vadun Service in Northern Haiti* (1940) or descriptions of the yearly festival cycle by many an anthropologist.

No simple categorization of these specific studies does justice to the variety and ingenuity of research now being undertaken. However, we can discuss some of the essential elements common among them. Before conducting research into a specific problem, an anthropologist must decide to limit himself in certain ways. He must ask himself: whether he will concentrate on answering some theoretical question provided by his discipline or give greatest emphasis to describing a set of related phenomena; whether he will work in urban, or rural, or suburban areas; whether he will include historical materials; whether he will stay in only one community or try to encompass a larger area; what techniques of information gathering he will use; whether he will emphasize his subjects' explanations or his own; whether he will try to devise experimental procedures; whether he will coordinate his research with other scholars; and to what extent he is willing to complicate his interpretation by considering the multitude of less immediate factors which impinge on his problem. These considerations are relevant whether he is interested in psychological, economic, sociological, religious, or other questions. The decisions the anthropologist makes regarding them must correspond both to the theories he will apply and to the goals he has set for himself. Many an anthropologist has not always been so clear about his field enterprise before he set out, but research in literate civilizations succeeds most fully when the strategies adopted make the two requirements of microscopic investigation and integrative generalization mutually supportive.

One good example of this is Clifford Geertz's study of Javanese religion (1960). As he writes in the introduction of his study,

> Java—which has been civilized longer than England; which in over a period of more than fifteen hundred years has seen Indians, Arabs, Chinese, Portuguese, and Dutch come and go; and which has today one of the world's densest populations, highest development of the arts, and most intensive agricultures—is not easily characterized under a single label or easily pictured in terms of a dominant theme. It is particularly true that in describing the religion of such a complex civilization as the Javanese any simple unitary view is certain to be inadequate (1960:7).

Geertz was faced with a twofold problem—not only was the diversity in Javanese religion geographical but there was also great religious diversity in the town in which he chose to live and study. How was he to describe the numerous varieties of practice and belief and still communicate the essential, common elements which tied them together and made them Javanese?

His solution was first to frankly acknowledge the differences he found. There were popular cults of many kinds, conservative and modern versions of Islam mysticism, and varieties of pseudo-religious political activity. His period of fieldwork was spent in a moderately large market and administrative center where a wide range of religious practices was represented. Using interviews, local records, some psychological projective techniques, and a great deal of direct observation, he gathered a rich body of detailed material. Geertz's efforts to integrate his material led him to show how variations in Javanese beliefs and practices correspond to social, educational, occupational, and other differences within the fabric of Javanese life. He illustrated how the various colors and hues of religion parallel and cross the other social contrasts within the society. Conflict and unity, whether of political action or religious belief, were shown to follow definite patterns and to be comprehensible to Western readers totally unfamiliar with Java. Geertz's primary concerns were to describe in detail and then to explain the place of religion in Javanese society. While he was no doubt very familiar with and interested in the specific questions about religious phenomena discussed within the social sciences, he did not tailor his research problem to answer any one of them.

Some anthropologists working in literate civilizations do precisely the opposite. They select a certain theoretical problem and utilize the materials available to formulate an answer. Take, for example, a study by Paul Friedrich (1964) of nineteenth-century Russian (European) kinship terminology. His primary aim, as he explains it, was "to examine interrelationships between patterns of social behavior and patterns of terminology" (1964:616). To do this he drew from the historical records and social histories whatever he felt was relevant to his problem and analyzed the material to discover semantic and behavioral patterns, which he then compared. He did not attempt a broad study of Russian kinship or the Russian language, but stayed very close to the theoretical problem before him. Unlike Geertz, Friedrich depended solely on written historical materials and did not go to Russia to do fieldwork—participant observation being, of course, out of the question in this case. The existence of a literate tradition, we should note, allows historical and "from-a-distance" studies, such as Friedrich's, which would be impossible for societies without written records.

Presuming sufficient uniformity across the hereditary occupationally based caste lines, Friedrich nevertheless confined himself to the central and especially the northern type of Russian dialects and cultures. Even here he found enormous variation in family size and composition:

> At one extreme, a separate hut might be occupied by one nuclear family of parents and children, particularly in the geographically peripheral western, southern and extreme northern regions. The middle range included many expanded families, especially stem families with a father and at least one married son. The other pole often presented the equivalent of large lineages, such as are found in patrilineal Tanala society. A great number of households had between twenty and thirty members; wealthy Cossak aggregates on the lower Don sometimes exceeded thirty; and Great Russian maxima in the forties are on record. The present study is not primarily concerned with the nuclear type or with the household corporations of over twenty-five (1964:138).

He concluded that the Russian kinship system conditioned the individual and his relatives in terms of household. Many relatives were emotionally and juridically differentiated and this differentiation was symbolized in kinship terminology. For example, "the component of the 'sex of linking relative' was related by implication to the household of birth and of post-marital identification, and the power of the household component was demonstrated by the way it overrode the component of generation" (Friedrich 1964:161). In reaching this conclusion Friedrich finds theoretic support in the work of W. H. R. Rivers (1914:78–81), who long ago postulated the "kindred" type of social organization especially typical of northeast European peasantry such as the Lithuanians. If Friedrich's idea that the Russian system as he has studied it resembles Rivers' kindred type of social organization is correct, we will then be able to link the Russian kinship system with all or most of those among northeast European peasantries. In addition Friedrich was able, on the basis of the kinship terminology, to compare and contrast the great Russian system with those of south India, Burma, the Coast

Salish, and the Huichol Indians. The need for the comparative perspective will be dealt with later. Other studies similar in scope and methods, though not done at a distance, are those on American kinship by Talcott Parsons (1943), Codere (1955), Schneider and Homans (1955), and Goodenough (1965).

Let us consider a very different kind of study from either of the preceding examples. Within anthropology there are numerous persons who have attempted or are attempting to test Western theories of psychology in non-Western societies. Theirs is a highly specialized kind of fieldwork often involving the application of personality tests or the use of depth personal interviews. Carstairs' psychoanalytic study (1957) of the three high castes (Brahmins, Rajputs, and Banias) in India's Rajasthan was confined to a single village with a secondary look, for comparative purposes, at another community of the Bhil tribe, living in the jungle valleys to the west. His main instrument was the depth interview, through which he obtained case histories from a total of 45 individuals. He also administered to each of his subjects the Rorschach test, a nonverbal intelligence test, and a word-association test. Without negating the shared historical, geographical, social, and economic influences which formed the "reality setting" of his subjects, Carstairs placed central emphasis on the role of infantile nuclear fantasies in the shaping of adult personality. He demonstrated that a number of Hindu personality traits would confound the Freudian psychologist. In Freudian psychology insistence upon fecal cleanliness is linked with obsessional characteristics such as punctuality, neatness, conscientiousness, and so on, but the Hindu in Carstairs' village exhibited contradictory characteristics with reference to Freud's "anal character,"—some directly in support of it, others directly opposed to it.

In making his study Carstairs chose not to emphasize the written material expressive of Hindu personality, but rather to concentrate on a small number of people in a single locality. Though his conclusions may have broad relevance to Indian society, he emphasized that what he described might not apply to Hindus elsewhere in India. In either case, however, he succeeded, as was his intention, in raising some theoretical questions about Freudian psychology by testing it in a culture very different from the one Freud and his patients knew in Vienna.

Some anthropologists have used a combination of sampling, questionnaire, intensive interviews, and tests to study a small segment of a large population or a particular aspect of the life of that segment of population. The anthropological interest in aging has expressed itself along such lines. A good example is that of Clark and Anderson, *Culture and Aging* (1967). They concentrated on 600 San Francisco people sixty years old and over, nearly evenly divided between the sexes, about half of whom were in the hospital at the time of study. They divided their data into two parts. The first consisted of questionnaire data and "scales, indices, ratings and scores derived from the examiner's observation of the subject, the subject's performance on certain tests and measurements, or his responses to a set of questions designed to measure some aspect of his cognitive, perceptual or emotional life" (Clark and Anderson 1967:75). The second part consisted of data derived from intensive study of the subjects three years later. In this part the two scholars attempted a "higher order of conceptualization" than in the first part (Clark and Anderson 1967:76).

Some of their results may come as a surprise to most Americans. For example, these anthropologists find a curious affinity in mental attitude between peasant society and the aged in San Francisco. This attitude is with reference to what Foster terms the "Image of Limited Good" (Foster 1965). By this "Image" Foster refers to a view on the part of peasants that all of the desired things in life—from land, wealth, health, and friendship to honor, respect, power, and influence—"exist in finite quantity and are always in short supply" as far as they are concerned. In addition, peasants feel that "there is no way directly within peasant power to increase the available quantities" (Foster 1965:296). Clark and Anderson feel that this peasant "Image" fits that of their "American aged" (Clark and Anderson 1967:430).

The one important difference between Clark and Anderson's study of the aged in San Francisco and the usual anthropological fieldwork in a village or tribe is that they did not live among the subjects nor interview the people forming part of the social milieu of the aged. Aging is another area of converging interest between anthropology and other disciplines, for the work of Anderson and Clark is not dissimilar to some studies carried out under the auspices of the Institute of Community Studies in London, for example, Townsend (1957 and 1963).

Evidently just as there are many ways of slicing the cultural pie, so there are numerous techniques among which anthropologists might choose for studying whatever aspect they select. My intention in this chapter has not been to provide complete coverage, but rather to exemplify by way of specific topics what has been and is being done. In the next two chapters we shall turn to the study of the small community as a whole or the national character as a whole.

4

Community Studies

GREAT CITIES, where the complex activities of government, religion, commerce, and art are centered, constitute one of the essential characteristics of literate civilizations. Most of the writings which constitute the traditions of literate civilizations have been made by citizens of these metropolises, and a class of urban intellectuals is usually most responsible for the continuity of these traditions. Consequently scholars in the humanities and social sciences turn most often to the cities and the literate traditions sponsored by them when they investigate literate civilizations. These metropolises, however, could not survive if it were not for the support they receive from the agricultural hinterlands which surround them. It is to the study of the people of the latter that many anthropologists have devoted themselves.

In agricultural areas the populations are relatively stable and the almost universal form of settlement is the small, local community from which the farmers daily may visit their fields, returning at night to the company of their fellow villagers. Studies of such settlements constitute the major portion of the community studies made by anthropologists. Today there are numerous extensions of the concept of community to a variety of groups (neighborhood, religious, ethnic, and so on) which exist within the confines of cities. Anthropologists occasionally study urban communities, but the term community study usually refers to the investigation of small, geographically discrete, rural settlements. This is the meaning to which we shall restrict our use here.

There is a very close relationship between the participant-observer method of research and the field of community studies, for if one is to observe closely the activities of a people (over an extended period), the group under observation will by necessity be a small one. The difference, then, between community studies and other kinds of participant research is that in a community study the goal is to describe how all of the various elements of the life of the people living in the community are integrated. Obviously a community study of a rural village can tell us only so much about the social and cultural life of the city dwellers of the

14

same civilization, yet to the extent that life in the villages and cities of a society are the same, village community studies often provide exceptionally clear illustrations of how the various elements of life fit together in the society. Even in instances in which community studies can tell us nothing of urban life, they do illuminate peasant society, which in most literate civilizations continues to contain the largest segment of the population.

Alan Beals states the case in another way in the introduction to his book on an Indian village:

> India contains not less than five hundred thousand villages. In these villages live approximately seven out of ten citizens of India, perhaps one out of every six or seven human beings in the world. The people who live in villages in India are inventive and conservative, tall and short, friendly and quarrelsome, handsome and ugly, wise and foolish, radical and reactionary. There are no typical rural Indians; there are no typical Indian villages. There are only human beings living in some relationship to the complex pattern of forces and ideas which constitute the civilization of India. To understand a single village and the people in it is to reach the beginning of an understanding of India—but it can be no more than a beginning. (Beals 1962)

Beals' point is well taken. It is a sound caution for students of community studies who claim "typicality" for their particular villages. The term typical often has been used too loosely by anthropologists and other social scientists. At the same time we must realize that there are physical limitations to what field investigators can cover with reference to hundreds of thousands of villages spread over a subcontinent (as distinguished from laboratory scientists dealing with hundreds or millions of specimens in a single room). Besides, there are urgent reasons (as we shall see later) why we must attempt to relate what we find in a single village to the larger national state and, in so doing, we must look for independent criteria upon which to judge the "typicality" of certain kinds of data uncovered in the local areas.

For example, I examined the kinship organization and the practices of and philosophy underlining ancestor worship in one locality in southwestern China. My conclusion was that in spite of a social and cultural pattern which would seem to protect the continuation of the social status of prominent families, this very system had built in it forces which favor the reverse trend. This mechanism for downward mobility was then seen as instrumental in the remarkable social mobility of traditional China as a whole (1948). The latter conclusion has since been confirmed in a number of studies by sociologists and historians (Hsu 1967b).

Robert Redfield was one of the first anthropologists to recognize the significance community studies might have to anthropology and to our understanding of literate civilizations. The questions with which he was concerned will serve to illustrate the place of community studies in the general context of the study of literate civilizations. Redfield went to the Mexican village of Tepoztlan in 1926 in order to investigate the effects of urban culture on rural society. He noted:

> The disorganization and perhaps the reorganization of the culture here considered under the slowly growing influence of the city is a process—a *diffusion* process— which can and will be studied. It is, the writer assumes, an example, within con-

venient limits, of the general type of change whereby primitive man becomes civilized man, the rustic becomes the urbanite" (1930:13–14).

He chose to look at Mexican culture from the perspective of an average village where modernization and social change were measured primarily in the acquisition of urban characteristics.[1] Redfield recognized that the village perspective was important for other reasons as well. First, community studies of peasants would fill a striking (when one thinks about it) void in our understanding of literate societies—the absence of any thorough knowledge of the lives being led by the masses of people living within the civilization's tradition, but, because they are either illiterate or inarticulate, not directly represented by it. In Mexico, for example, Mexico City is more European than Indian, yet the majority of villages represent traditions more Indian than European. Indian traditions make village life quite distinct from that of the city and they profoundly influence the peasants' understanding of whatever the city offers them. Without the village perspective we would be likely to conclude either that all of Mexico was similar to Mexico City or that the peasants maintained a way of life totally different from the urban one. Detailed community studies have made it possible to appreciate the actual interrelationships between rural and urban modes of life and between Indian and European influences.

Second, Redfield also wished to emphasize the contemporary in rural society. Anthropologists before him had often been interested in peasant life because in it were preserved many ancient "folk" traditions, but for Redfield, just as for the villagers themselves, everything that went on was important for it was all part of the experience of living in Tepoztlan.

Third, he was to stress in his later writings on community studies—one which we have already mentioned several times—the necessity of studying the village in its totality. He recognized that there are many ways of conceiving of the whole entity that is a community; and he was aware that many forms for expressing the way the various parts fit together could be used. He wrote of the different kinds of models of integration one might introduce, depending on what elements were given central importance in the analysis. The small community, for him, was the ideal place to scientifically explore the functional interrelationships between the different aspects of human society.

Since Redfield, a number of anthropologists dealing with literate civilizations have greatly amplified and extended our views of localized studies or made them more precise. Leach, in connection with his work on a village in Ceylon (1961), stressed the distinction between two distinct classes of social facts "which call for fundamentally different techniques of investigation" because they are not of the same order of significance. The essentially statistical facts such as birthrates, production rates, living standards, and so forth, are of local significance. These particulars, however detailed, cannot be the basis for generalization on "an entire region," but in the field of law "particular instances, actual precedents,"

---

[1] If we were to measure change in Tepoztlan today, we would be inclined to emphasize things other than city traits, such as technological progress, social mobility, and labor migration.

are even more crucial than the general principles (Leach 1961:4). Wolf explicated the differences between local informal groups which are relevant to the larger societal organization and others which are not. Speaking of "kinship friendship and patron-client relationships" in Middle America, Wolf noted that, "Sometimes such informal groupings cling to the formal structure like barnacles to a rusty ship. At other times informal social relations are responsible for the metabolic processes required to keep the formal institution operating, as in the case of armies locked in combat" (Wolf 1966:2).

The problem of relating the details from a single community to the larger civilization of which it is a part will engage our attention later (Chapter 7). In the meantime we shall turn to studies of national character.

5

National Character Studies

THE NEED FOR RELATING the village to its larger social and cultural context is inevitable. The practical side of this need is in keeping with the theoretical side of it. The need remains whether we take the older view of culture as the "historically created designs for living, explicit and implicit, rational, irrational and non-rational, which exist at any given time as potential guides for the behavior of men," each "historically derived system of . . . designs" tending "to be shared by all or specifically designated members of a group" (Kluckhohn and Kelly 1945:97–98), or the more recent view of culture as the "organization of diversity," as "policy, tacitly and gradually concocted by groups of people for the furtherance of their interests; also contract, established by practice, between and among individuals to organize their strivings into mutually facilitating equivalence structures" (Wallace 1961:28). The anthropological significance of the patterns of life in a village must be understood in some perspective of the larger society as a whole.

To have spelled out the need for relating the microscosm to the macrocosm is one thing; to do it satisfactorily is quite another. National character studies constitute one answer to this need. It is not generally appreciated that the first attempt at characterizing whole peoples other than on the basis of their physical characteristics was by Pitt-Rivers in a book entitled *Clash of Culture and Contact of Races* (1927). He described the Australian aborigines as "introvert," as contrasted to native Africans, who were "extrovert." He then sought in this dichotomy to explain why the former were dying out while the latter were physically prospering. Benedict's *Patterns of Culture* (1934) was the book which clearly ushered in the trend of national character studies more definitively, even though the book does not concern itself with literate societies.[1] In this work Benedict contrasted the Zuñi Indians with the Kwakiutl Indians and the Dobuans of the South

---

[1] Nonanthropologists de Tocqueville (*The American Democracy,* 1862, 1945) and de Madariaga (*Englishmen, Frenchmen, Spaniards: An Essay in Comparative Psychology,* 1928) both came before this.

Seas. The former she called "Apollonian" because of the restraint in their interpersonal relations, the submergence of the individual in the group, their slowness to anger, and the absence of "hysteria" in their religious rites, and the like. The latter two she called "Dionysian." The extravagant and wasteful rites that characterized the Kwakiutl potlatch, their need for "avenging" any death in the kinship group by the wanton killing of a victim outside of their group on the assumption that any death in "my" family is an act of malice on the part of someone else, the Dobuans' use of garden magic and other acts to extend the personality and establish the ego—these and many other patterns of customary behavior were seen as Dionysian. Margaret Mead's *Coming of Age in Samoa* (1928) was probably the first anthropological work that made specific comparisons between a tribal society and a large literate society (the United States) in terms of their differing experiences in adolescence.[2] However, it was Mead's *And Keep Your Powder Dry* (1942, 1965) on America and Benedict's *The Chrysanthemum and the Sword* (1946) on Japan that truly set in full swing the anthropological study of national character of literate societies.

Mead is of the opinion that, "although the national-character approach utilizes the premises and methods of the personality and culture field, historically it has had two distinguishing features: the group of persons with shared social tradition is selected for study because they are the citizens or subjects—the "nationals"—of a sovereign political state, and the society *may* be so inaccessible to direct field observation that less direct methods of research have to be used" (Mead 1962:396). Benedict's work on Japan illustrates both of these features, but Mead's own work on America fits only the first of the two.

The central attempt of the national character approach is to relate as many institutions of any culture with some over-all pattern, according to the Apollonian-Dionysian or introvert-extrovert contrasts, or some other scheme. In the case of Benedict's study of the Japanese a major point that concerned her was why the Japanese could be so cruel toward prisoners of war, but also be so cooperative and respectful toward the conquerors after Japan's total defeat. Judging by Japanese behavior before and during World War II, many Americans feared that the Japanese would be "sullen and hostile, a nation of watchful avengers who might sabotage any peaceful program," but their fears were proven to be unfounded. The Japanese after defeat seemed to turn into a nation of new men with complete individual acceptance of the defeat and pledged good faith under a new democratic national policy.

Benedict describes Japan's strength as the tendency to proceed singlemindedly and with her full power in one direction, but, when that course of action fails, to proceed with equal determination in the opposite direction. "The Japanese have an ethic of alternatives. They tried to achieve their 'proper place' in war and they lost. That course, now, they can discard, because their whole training has conditioned them to possible changes of direction" (1946:304). This ability to turn about face without remorse is, according to Benedict, rooted in the growing up experiences of the Japanese individual.

---

[2] Her comparisons were later on greatly amplified in her book *Male and Female* (1949) in which she drew on data from seven sea tribes and US society.

The contradictions which all westerners have described in Japanese character are intelligible from their child rearing. It produces a duality in their outlook on life neither side of which can be ignored. From their experiences of privilege and psychological ease in babyhood they retain through all the disciplines in later life the memory of an easier life when they "did not know shame". . . . Gradually, after they are six or seven, responsibility for circumspection and "knowing shame" is put upon them and upheld by the most drastic of sanctions; their own family will turn against them if they default (Benedict 1946:286–287).

Mead's *And Keep Your Powder Dry* (1942, 1965) delineated the American character as one that

is geared to success and to movement, invigorated by obstacles and difficulties, but plunged into guilt and despair by catastrophic failure or a wholesale alteration in the upward and onward pace; a character in which aggressiveness is uncertain and undefined, to which readiness to fight anyone who starts a fight and unreadiness to engage in violence have both been held up as virtues; a character which measures its successes and failures only against near contemporaries and engages in various quantitative devices for reducing every contemporary to its own stature; a character which sees success as the reward of virtue and failure as the stigma for not being good enough; a character which is uninterested in the past, except when ancestry can be used to make points against other people in the success game; a character oriented towards an unknown future, ambivalent towards other cultures, which are regarded with a sense of inferiority as more coherent than our own and with a sense of superiority because newcomers in America display the strongest mark of other cultural membership in the form of foreignness (1965:193–194).

This American character is, according to Mead, generated in a family constellation in which the "third generation" psychology prevails, in which parents expect their children's achievements to be different from their own, and sibling rivalry is high. This same American character propelled the American way of prosecuting the war (World War II) with a peculiar American expectation of building the world anew after the conclusion of the war (Mead 1965:193–250).

Some other works which deal with various national characters with varying scope (some being mission oriented and some not dealing with childhood experiences) but more or less the same methodology are as follows: Brickner, *Is Germany Incurable?* (1943); Lowie, *The German People, A Social Portrait to 1914* (1945); Gorer, *The American People* (1948); Gorer and Rickman, *The People of Great Russia* (1962); Riesman *The Lonely Crowd* (1950); Wolfenstein and Leites, *Movies, A Psychological Study* (1950); Mead, *Soviet Attitudes Toward Authority* (1951); Hsu, *Americans and Chinese* (1955); Lowie, *Toward Understanding Germany* (1954); Gorer, *Exploring English Character* (1955); and Haring, *Personal Character and Cultural Milieu* (1956).[3]

Previously, we mentioned that the central attempt of the national character approach is to relate as many institutions of any culture as possible with some over-all pattern. We now must add that most national character studies are often

---

[3] Though Haring's is a collection of essays, a number of the essays deal with the national character of Japan..

predicated on the assumption that childhood experiences, or at least the early family constellations in which the individual finds himself, have a great deal to do with the formation of a personality orientation which then is congruent with the over-all pattern of the culture. This linkage which is assumed may be roughly schematized as follows:

(A) Childhood experiences ——> (B) Personality formation ——>
(C) Over-all culture pattern of the society

Some anthropologists are more extreme than others. For example, Bateson suggests that British and American colonial attitudes are extensions of their respective parent-child relationships. The American parents encourage their children to "certain sorts of boastful and exhibitionistic behavior while still in a position somewhat subordinate to and dependent upon the parents," while in England the parent-child relationship is characterized by "dominance and succoring." The American parent-child relationship "contains within itself factors for psychologically weaning the child, while in England, among the upper classes, the analogous breaking of the succoring-dependence link has to be performed by . . . the boarding school." Since "colonies cannot be sent to a boarding school," therefore "England has very great difficulty in weaning her non-Anglo-Saxon colonies, while these colonies have had corresponding difficulty in attaining maturity—in sharp contrast with the history of the Philippines" (Bateson 1942:76–82).

Geoffrey Gorer gives an equally daring analysis when he maintains that the sibling relationship in the American family is of no great importance with only one "important exception." This occurs:

. . . when two children of the same sex, particularly two boys are born within a short interval of each other. . . . The elder brother is likely to introduce the younger brother into his play groups, and later his gang. . . . The younger brother is a member of a group in the majority older than he is, and with standards of daring and accomplishment beyond the level of his years. Fired by the standard he is set, the younger brother becomes extravagantly rash in his words and actions, confident that he will be saved from the dangerous results of his behavior by his older brother's protections, by his superior strength and wisdom.

He concludes,

This situation is common enough to have several analogues in adult life. The most striking is to be seen in Congress, where the House of Representatives often acts most irresponsibly, in the confidence that its elder brother, the Senate, will save it from the worst aspects of its folly (1948:96).

An observation of this sort is of very little scientific worth. It is almost in the same class as the kind of argument which attempts to link the appearance and disappearance of sunspots with the business cycle. There is an enormously wide gulf between the two phenomena in the supposed linkage which Gorer has not bothered to bridge.

What needs to be seen is that, although the growing up experiences of the individual indubitably have something to do with the social and cultural behavior of the adult world, the relationship is not a simple one. Any attempt to seize upon a single item in the former to explain most or all of the latter will lead to little more than wild speculation. The "Swaddling hypothesis," first propounded by Gorer and Rickman in their portrait of the Russian character (1962), is another such example. In this regard what Mead says about the swaddling hypothesis is more scientifically acceptable than expressions given it by its original authors:

> The statement is not *swaddling makes Russians.* It is: *From an analysis of the way Russians swaddle infants, it is possible to build a model of Russian character formation which enables us to relate what we know about human behavior and what we know about Russian culture in such a way that Russian behavior becomes more understandable* (Mead 1954:401–402) (italics Mead's).

From this point of view the relationships among childhood experiences, personality characteristics, and pattern of the society's culture are better represented as follows:

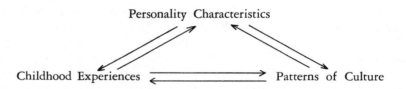

We must eschew extreme simplification and see the growing-up experiences of the individual and the patterns of adult behavior in broader relationships. Specific mechanisms such as swaddling or discontinuity in discipline (severity before indulgence or vice versa) are part of a larger kinship constellation, which may embody the same basic principles upon which the entire society and culture are built. The same principles will not merely be seen as linking some particular item in childhood experience with another particular corresponding one in adult behavior in a one to one relationship, but may be seen as manifesting themselves in diverse ways in all three clusters although, in each new generation, the childhood experiences reintroduce, reinforce, or even escalate the same principles.

This was the general sense in which Mead (1942, 1965) related the broader American family constellation to the American character in general; Spindler related it to the American attitude toward military requirements and restrictions (1948); and I related the differences between the American and Chinese family constellations to the differences between the contrasting ways in which the two peoples have reacted to men, gods, and things (1955).

There is a particular group of students who approach the study of literate (and nonliterate) civilizations very differently. They are bent on identifying the universal elements in the human psyche and, in the process, generally make what may be termed psychoanalyses of entire societies. Géza Róheim was one of the most important instigators of this approach and he has not a few followers. These are persons well steeped in psychoanalysis but much less versed in the social sciences. Furthermore, as Schneider put it, "social phenomena appear to be a kind of plaything to exercise their art without responsibility" (1956:953). Róheim's own work in this regard was best exemplified in his book *Psychoanalysis and Anthropology* (1950) in which he took into account the Aranda culture of central Australia (where he resided for fourteen months), the Dobuan culture of Normanby Island in the South seas (where he resided for nine months), the Alor of Timor, the Yurok and Navaho Indians of North America, the Kaingang of the highlands of Brazil, the Marquesan culture in the Pacific Ocean, and contemporary Hungary (both peasants and their overlords).

Though his results definitely came within the scope of the national character approach (in that he attempted to ascertain the relationship between the parts and the whole in literate as well as nonliterate societies), Róheim was antagonistic to it. He was interested in demonstrating that the Oedipus Complex exists everywhere with some minor variation in detail. He was primarily interested in the universal psychic foundations especially that of the unconscious which, according to him, are similar in all societies. He objected to national character studies by anthropologists on two grounds. First, anthropological attempts to ascertain culturally or socially determined differences in national character sprang from their "ethnocentrism," and they often used the concept of "cultural relativity" to cover up their real attitude toward other societies—"you are completely different but I forgive you" (1950:362). Second, he thought it was not only wrong to study the differences between societies but also that when it comes to modern nations the facts are so complex that no over-all patterns can be arrived at. As evidence for the latter he cited the example of peasant Hungary where every region seems to differ from every other region in child rearing, in sex mores, in the position of the old vis-à-vis the young, and so on (1950:369–386).

However, his sources of information even about Hungarian culture and society were open to serious question. For example, he asked himself the following question: "Is there a common childhood situation in Hungary?" He then answered himself: "Luckily we have a booklet written on the basis of questionnaires by an obstetrician long before psychoanalysis was invented" (1950:369). (The booklet was published in 1911.) Or again: "Tard, a palòck (subgroup of the Hungarians, probably of Kumanian origin) village in northern Hungary, although they too have their troubles, shows a much healthier situation. *I happen to know something about this village because I analyzed a man who had grown up there*" (1950:376) (italics mine).

Followers of Róheim have published a large number of books and articles among which are *Psychoanalysis and Culture: Essays in Honor of Géza Róheim* (edited by Wilbur and Muensterberger 1951), a series of volumes entitled *Psychoanalysis and the Social Sciences* founded by Róheim, continued with Muensterberger and Axelrad as its editors (1947–1958; and superseded by *The Psychoanalytic Study of Society*, 1960 to present). While Róheim went on from one region of Hungary to another noting the wide differences, Muensterberger seems to regard an impressionistic reaction to a large population like that of China as important evidence for the psychoanalysis of the Chinese society and culture as a whole. The following is a good illustration of how some of these people go about their tasks. In a piece on "Orality and Dependence Among the

Chinese," Muensterberger says that "the oral-sadistic tendencies" among Chinese women "are maintained and reinforced by the complementary emotions of the Chinese male. They are often prompted by the projections of men who fear or try to avoid genital contact with the mother substitute." His entire evidence for these "projections" rests on the following:

> In a personal conversation, the Sinologist Dr. Karl A. Wittfogel wittily commented upon this trait: "If he (the Chinese) cannot eat, he sublimates by fornicating" (1951:65).

One cannot imagine any scholar using such a supposed witticism as serious evidence for any aspect of American character, such as a notion that the American males "fear or try to avoid genital contact with the mother substitute." Yet Muensterberger apparently regards this as such a very important datum about the Chinese that, five years later, he used it again, this time in support of his thesis that the Chinese social organization demands solidarity among the family members and that such demands create tension which is relieved by close mother-son ties and unlimited feeding (1955:18). The manner in which Muensterberger uses the same datum on these two different occasions is probably also significant. On the first occasion, Dr. Wittfogel was simply designated a "Sinologist," and the datum was given in a footnote, but on the later occasion he was a "well known Sinologist" and the same words are part of the main text.

Fortunately for the science of man, this free-for-all way of approaching national character is not generally too influential. It is quite overshadowed by the intellectually more sophisticated approach represented by Kardiner and Linton. Two major publications have resulted from this collaboration: *The Individual and His Society* (Kardiner in association with Ralph Linton 1939) and *Psychological Frontiers of Society* (Kardiner in collaboration with Linton, DuBois, and West 1945). Though the major parts of these two works deal with nonliterate societies, the second publication also deals with "Plainville, U.S.A." (pseudonym of a village in Missouri), as presented by James West (whom we have mentioned before). The Kardiner-Linton central conceptual tool is the basic personality type which, "for any society is that personality configuration which is shared by the bulk of the society's members as a result of the early experiences which they have in common" (Linton, Foreword, *Psychological Frontiers of Society* 1945: viii). As Linton explained it:

1. That the individual's early experiences exert a lasting affect upon his personality, especially upon the development of his projective systems.
2. That similar experiences will tend to produce similar personality configurations in the individuals who are subjected to them.
3. That the techniques which the members of any society employ in the care and rearing of children are culturally patterned and will tend to be similar, although never identical, for various families within the society.
4. That the culturally patterned techniques for the care and rearing of children differ from one society to another.

If these postulates are correct, and they seem to be supported by a wealth of evidence, it follows:

1. That the members of any given society will have many elements of early experience in common. .
2. That as a result of this they will have many elements of personality in common.
3. That since the early experience of individuals differs from one society to another, the personality norms for various societies will also differ. (Kardiner and associates 1945:vii–viii).

Equipped with the concept of basic personality type or structure, Kardiner describes the childhood experiences which enter into it as primary institutions, while religion and folklore are secondary institutions. The central idea is that the former creates something in the individual which forms the basis for the projective systems subsequently used to create folklore and religion (Kardiner and associates 1945:23–24).

On this basis Kardiner analyzes the culture of Plainville, U.S.A., and from that goes on to the United States culture as a whole. He finds in Plainville child experiences a good maternal care which leads to "strong attachment to and idealization of the mother as guardian and helper in distress, an attitude easily extended to the father when the child is able to recognize his importance." "This lays a strong foundation for strong social cohesion, and for cooperation." But this favorable situation in infancy is considerably distorted by later disciplines "which help the process of growth in some respects but introduce painful factors in others. . . . The painful factors are introduced chiefly in the sexual development." Kardiner summarizes:

> Some of the socially relevant outcomes of the basic personality structure must be stressed. Though the emerging individual has a high emotional potential, too many blocked-action systems are created. The capacity for idealization, and hence worship, of "great men" is created, as well as the foundation for a religion with an idealized deity with great power for both good and harm. On the other hand, from the blocked systems we derive (a) serious sexual disturbances, both on the affective and executive side (potency); (b) great variations in aggression patterns, with psychosomatic accompaniments; (c) marked variations in the attitude to authority, excessive submission and passivity (even to the extent of dragging in the sexual organization in the form of homosexuality, asceticism, or perversion); or excessive and premature independence (paranoid personalities) (1945:376).

Kardiner regards this type of basic personality orientation as containing the seeds for social instability in which, on the one hand, the struggle for success becomes a most powerful force because it is the equivalent of self-preservation and self-esteem, but, on the other, failing that, and even while struggling for that, the individual is isolated "because he is prevented from building friendly relationships" due to "mutual hostilities" as a matter of self-defense, which in turn perpetuates a "class" system "in which everyone is obliged to safeguard his self-esteem by having social relations only with those who can act as mirrors to his affective self." This is the basic motive for "exclusiveness, snobbishness, cliques, clubs, neighborhoods, race hatred, and the like." (1945:411–412).

From this analysis of culture and personality of Plainville, U.S.A., and then America, Kardiner enters into a brief exploration of the history of the West. The two basic factors underlying the Western basic personality are: good maternal care and the repression of sexual impulses. The interplay of these two found expression in Calvinism, which solved this problem by "giving free rein to those forms of aggression that were compatible to the new goal of social well-being and at the same time retained the strictest control over the pleasure drive." This "inordinate control of pleasure drives was unconsciously interpreted as a form of cruelty, which in turn has to lead to either masochistic or externalized form of cruelty." Consequently, success was interpreted as reward, but, by the same token, failure could be seen as punishment. However, "if the individual interprets his failure as an evidence of inadequacy or of not being loved then he may feel himself absolved of the necessity for all impulse control. . . . Then "the internalized conscience fails and the social control passes from the internalized discipline to dominance-submission polarity weighed on a plane of coercion, forcible elimination of competition, or even annihilation." (1945:451–453).

It will be noted that nearly all of these national character studies were done in the 1950s or earlier. Is this approach no longer in vogue and, if so, why? I think the answer to the first part of the question is yes, and the reasons are not too obscure. Anthropological research, like other activities, has tended to wax and wane around different themes or areas at different times. Evolution and diffusion were each, at one time or another, the primary concern of anthropology, but evolution dropped in popularity for a long time, and diffusion has become no more than a commonplace minor issue today.

National character studies received their greatest impetus from World War II. "Anthropologists found themselves personally and directly involved in the international situation, both as citizens and scientists" (Hunt 1965:138). The need in general for knowing what kind of people the Japanese, the Germans, and, later, the Russians were led many anthropologists into the attempt to ascertain the behavior of these and other large national groups as wholes. As the war ended and as Americans poured into Japan and Germany as reformers, teachers, and researchers without the psychological pressures and urgency of the war, but with much greater opportunities for individual contacts with some of these peoples, some of the pictures of the wholes were punctured by details which seemingly contradicted them. At least the wholes were no longer such neat entities as before. The desire to study the parts prevailed over the need to understand the wholes.

The latter fact also meshed well with the greater emphasis on methodology culminating in the postwar emphasis on cross-cultural correlation on a wide scale and computerization.

A temporary drop of enthusiasm for national character studies among anthropologists is no reason to presume their total demise. Evolution as an issue has more recently been revived (White 1959; Sahlins 1960) and, in my view, will again occupy a more prominent place in anthropological researches for some time to come. A more spectacular new development is the relationship between physical anthropology and social anthropology. A few years back physical anthropology was nearly synonymous with the study of racial characteristics or human body types—at best, blood types. When anthropologists found race (however sophisticated its definition) could not be scientifically linked with such things as cultural vicissitudes or somatotype to adolescent delinquency, they lost interest. Now physical anthropology has a new link with social (maybe also psychological) anthropology by way of primate studies.

But national character studies have not suffered from total anthropological eclipse. Some anthropologists may not agree with me, but I think a most recent example of such a study is that by Jules Henry (*Culture Against Man*, 1963). In the national character studies mentioned so far childhood experiences (if dealt with at all) figure largely. They are seen as the arena in which the individual receives messages which then enable him to play his part as an adult adequately in accordance with the larger patterns of culture of his society. The emphasis is on the similarity between childhood experiences and adult behavior. Henry's work is within this broad scope, but he gives special emphasis, as did Fromm before him (1941), to what the American culture pattern, with its economic structure centered in material greatness and conflicting values, has done to the American national character, parent-child relations, teen-age problems, the schools, emotional well-being, and old age. Henry says that his "*is not an objective description of America*, but rather a passionate ethnography" (1963:3). His central concern is with the American "national character in a culture increasingly feeling the effects of almost 150 years of lopsided preoccupation with amassing wealth and raising its standard of living" (1963:4–5). And his data are those from the usual anthropological observation, participation, and interview, but perhaps rather more than the usual amount of biographical sources.

What Henry sees is a culture which drives relentlessly toward more desire, planned obsolescence, forced separation between the job and the self on the part of the majority,[4] a spreading fear of "competition, of failure, of loss of markets, of humiliation, of becoming obsolete . . ., of the boss" all the way to "fear of the Soviet Union" (1963:41). Hard pressed by so harsh a cultural reality, Americans old or young, sick or healthy, engage in "fun" with a vengeance, as a matter of "adaptive radiation" (1963:13–44).

Henry then examines the relations between American parents and children and among children, and, finally, the mental and social world of the aged, and finds that all of these reflect the consequences of the particular American institutional dynamics—a society so vigorously engaged in surviving physically may also be dying emotionally.

---

[4] What Henry speaks of as "separation between the job and the self" may be really a lack of focus that could integrate the different aspects of peoples' lives.

6

Some Problems

WE HAVE ROUGHLY DIFFERENTIATED four kinds of works on literate civilizations: those which deal with some aspects of each, such as art or mythology; those which concentrate on the personality characteristics of a limited number of individuals, for which generalizations about the entire group are made; those which confine themselves to a single village or community; and those which attempt to cover each civilization as a whole by unraveling the underlying unitary characteristics. Some of these studies link literate civilizations with non-literate societies because their methodology or conceptual tools derived from the latter. But many of them do not.

Class, Caste, and Regional Differences

Now we must deal with some of the general problems. One of these concerns class, caste, and regional differences which may be obvious in many literate societies. How can conclusions based on data gathered from one segment be relevant to other segments of the society? The Hindu Brahman can accept food or water from very few fellow men, but a Hindu belonging to a subcaste designated as some sort of Sudra can accept nourishment from a much wider circle of mankind. A member of the Chinese literati usually has separate tablets for many more generations of lineal ancestors in his household shrine, in contrast to a Chinese coolie, who usually posts no more than a sheet of red paper with an inscription representing in composite form only three lineal forebears and their spouses.[1] The

---

[1] Since the Chinese Communist Revolution of 1949 and the wide publicity given its many spectacular and often brutal techniques for promoting change, there is a popular notion that the Chinese society and culture have been entirely changed from their traditional condition into something different. Consequently, the reader may question the validity of speaking of any aspect of Chinese traditional patterns of life in the present tense. What we need to realize is that all non-Western societies have been under more or less pressure for changes of Western origin of one variety or another. Some of them have changed more than others. The Chinese have been undergoing this process since 1840. The process of change was more accelerated after each political change from the Sun Yat-Sen led 1912 Republican

branch houses (*bunke*) are much more tied and subordinated to the main houses (*honke*) in northern and central Japan than in western and southwestern Japan. We can go on enumerating these differences indefinitely.

I think these differences are important, but still do not prevent the student from identifying the unifying features of each civilization in spite of them. For example, it is a well-established fact that while the Chinese have traditionally given much social fanfare to the "big family" ideal, field investigations showed the actual number of families with several generations under the same roof to be very small. Furthermore, it was also unmistakable that the big families with several generations under the same roof were much more likely to be found among the affluent and the socially prominent than among the poor and the common men. But the poor did not have a different culture. On the contrary, it can be demonstrated that size of household rose directly with the increase of social status. That this is not merely due to the higher infant survival rate among the rich was attested to by the fact that the bigger families were bigger not because of the number of surviving children but because of the presence of a larger number of collateral relatives (Hsu 1943). In other words, the cultural model of higher and lower classes was the same, but the latter could only move toward that model when economic conditions permitted.

The differences in custom between the higher and lower caste Hindus tend to be more striking than between the classes in China. Because of this fact, we must especially guard against failure to see the forest for the trees. The differential behavior patterns of the low-caste Chamars and the high-caste Thakurs of the village of Senapur in Uttar Pradesh, northern India, will serve to illustrate an important point. Under modern impact the Chamars are observed to be moving toward greater traditionalization, while the Thakurs tend toward greater Westernization (Cohn 1961).

On the surface, there are contradictory patterns of behavior here, but the incompatibilities are more superficial than real. They can easily be reconciled if we examine them in a wider perspective and introduce the concepts of status seeking and time lag.

The low-caste Chamars of Senapur move toward greater traditionalization as a result of modernizing forces such as literacy and urban experience because they, like their low-caste brethren elsewhere, wish to raise their status wherever and whenever they feel they can do something about it. The means to which they resort in this status-raising effort are strongly determined by their model of high status. They will move toward greater traditionalization as a means (whether it is forbidding widow remarriage or creation of a fictitious Brahmanic past) as long as the modernizing forces have stimulated their aspirations, but have not made any inroads on their model of high status.

revolution onwards. The 1949 communist revolution was but a more extreme successor of those movements which preceded it. However, on the one hand, the communist regime has not completely changed the traditional patterns of life even in mainland China. Otherwise, it would have no need for the many continuing antilandlord antientrepreneur, anti-intellectual movements of which the latest was exemplified by the Red Guards. On the other hand, the kind of pattern described here is clearly visible in Taiwan today and, I am sure, still to be found in mainland China for years to come if we had the opportunity for direct observation.

The Thakurs also wish to raise their status, or at least to maintain it, but being way above the Chamars on the caste hierarchy, economically better off and more powerful, the Thakurs have had more opportunity for contact with modernizing forces, and their model of high status has already been affected by some of the modernizing forces, including those originating from Western missionaries and Hindus who have had Western education.

Yet a group can no more completely abandon its past than can an individual. In seeking a modernized model of high status the Thakurs have to use the old as well as the new. As time rolls on and as modernizing forces expand their spheres of influence, the attainable model of high status for the low-caste Chamars may well merge into some of the modernized features currently associated with the Thakur model. When that happens, we can expect the Chamars, too, to move toward status symbols which are mixtures of modernization and traditionalization. This seems already to have occurred in the village of Rampur on the outskirts of Delhi. Here the high-caste Jats, like their Thakur counterparts in Senapur, have become more Westernized in their outlook and behavior. The Chamars of Rampur have sought to raise their status by moving in two directions. On one hand, they have adopted traditional status symbols by abandoning such polluting practices as removing dead animals, skinning hides, and eating meat. On the other hand, they have utilized modern avenues of status mobility by participating in the national Congress party and demanding modern education for their children (Lewis 1958:62–79).

These processes have been and are being repeated, with more or less intensity, in various societies in transition (see also Srinivas 1955–1956:492–496), but will be difficult to perceive until we raise our sights from the localized particulars. The Senapur situation just described is no more than another instance in which the higher and the lower strata of a population share the same model of social advancement, the only difference being that the lower group is resorting to status symbols which the higher group is partially abandoning in favor of some newer symbols, but the basic aspiration of upward movement in a caste hierarchy is the same.

The class and Negro-white differences in the United States have been the object of much sociological and some anthropological literature. They have differential access to power and the good life. There are men and women who have inherited great wealth and others who have had to start from scratch. The latter distinction is very interesting in light of the revelation by Warner and associates that inherited money is rated above earned money (Warner 1949:39–42). There are class differences in child rearing; the middle class young are enjoined to defer gratification much more than their peers situated in the lower strata of society (Honigmann 1954:316–320). The Kinsey reports (1948, 1953) reveal class differences in sex behavior. However, the importance of these differences must not be overestimated or in any case allowed to obscure our views of the underlying tendency toward uniformity. For example, according to a *Fortune* poll in 1940, most Americans regard themselves as belonging to the "middle class." (This is significant even though the outcome depended in part on the way the survey question was worded.) It is a well-known fact that, as Negro-Americans become more affluent, many tend to adopt American "middle class" mores (though some will expressly reject them). The more recent civil rights movements and disturbances show that a majority of unprivileged Americans are no longer content to be forced to live differently. In a society where mail-order houses reach the most remote villages, where movies and other public communication media are common in all regions, where public education is universal, and where freedom and equality are its founding ideals, different strata of the population are much more likely to share the same cultural model for advancement than those areas where such conditions do not exist.

In this situation there could well be (and often are) more than one or two models for advancement within any society at any given point of time (no society is completely homogeneous), but the processes and the over-all direction or directions are ascertainable. Once we have adequate knowledge of how the elite group or groups function, we are fairly sure of being able to understand the aspirational direction or directions of the villagers and others situated below them. Variations in any organized society are not random. All their significant varieties are not irrelevant to the central cultural system exemplified in the patterns of conduct on the part of the elite. Even when a literate society is pulled asunder by internal revolution, it is usually some section of the elite that provides the masses with new direction. For example, there is ample evidence that the leaders of both the Nationalist and the Communist movements in modern Chinese history "have been drawn most frequently from a relatively thin upper layer of the Chinese population. In both parties these men were often the sons of landlords, merchants, scholars, or officials, and they usually came from parts of China where Western influence had first penetrated and where the penetration itself was most vigorous" (North 1952:46–47).

"Sampling" Problem

A second problem is size of sample. This is the most common of all criticisms leveled against studies of literate civilizations, but especially against national character studies. How can one obtain enough adequate samples to generalize about large nations like the United States, Russia, or China? How can we talk about a U.S. culture when we know that there are Americans of diverse ethnic backgrounds and religious persuasions? In connection with village or community studies in large literate civilizations, some scholars have even pleaded that we must wait for more such works before making any over-all generalizations about any society, region, or people. They dwell on the complexity of each society, on the variations in details, and, in the case of India, seem to think that all generalizations about Hindu India are a long way off. These scholars have not reflected on two facts. First, there are about 500,000 villages in India. Even if we can expect 50 village studies a year, it would take 10 centuries to complete 10 percent of the Indian villages, by which time the earlier monographs would most likely need a great deal of revision before they could be used for synthesis with the later products. The task is simply impossible.

The matter of coverage, however, is strictly relative. Previously, we noted that nonliterate societies vary enormously in size from a few hundred to many millions and that most of them are not as homogeneous as the anthropologist's approach has appeared to make them out to be. Yet even in the smaller ones, the question of adequate coverage is always problematic. For example, Honigmann (1949) obtained among the Kaska Indians not more than 6 brief life histories and only 28 Rorschach protocols among a population of 175. Oscar Lewis' (1951) refutation of Redfield's characterization of Tepotzlán in Mexico was primarily based upon usable Rorschach protocols of 100 individuals and intensive data on 7 families in a population of 4000. DuBois (1944) obtained life histories of 8 Alorese and 37 Rorschach protocols of others in a population of less than 160 in a larger cluster of villages including about 600.

What DuBois says of her 8 autobiographies of so small a population is very interesting:

> The persons from whom autobiographies were secured do not represent the ideal or "type" person of Atimelang. The most successful men said they were too busy with their financial and ceremonial affairs to spend the time required for telling a life history. Actually they probably did not need either the fee or the prestige that working with me involved. The "ideal" women of Atimelang, of whom there were a few, were either too unassertive or too engrossed in work to come daily to my house. I am under the impression that inability to secure autobiographical material from the successful type of individuals of a culture is an experience many ethnographers have had in functioning societies. However, the autobiographies given here do represent, on the whole, average Atimelang adults. Of the eight, Fantan, Malelaka, and Lomani are farthest from the norm (DuBois 1944:191).

We do not dispute that these 8 "represent, on the whole, average Atimelang adults," but if successful Alorese men "did not need either the fee or the prestige that working with" an anthropologist involved, how much less would the successful American men need "the fee or the prestige" in a similar situation?

These facts are pointed out not to justify the present state of affairs, but to underscore the lack of any clearly agreed upon criterion for judging the intensity of anthropological field studies. Lacking such a criterion, the one that we presently employ to evaluate the worth of a given field study is primarily qualitative: the fullness of the descriptive material, the extent of internal consistency, the training of the fieldworker, the conditions under which his fieldwork was carried out, and, in general, how his results compare with other results from a similar area. Some reports may provide more details than others, but there is no reason to suppose that details as such are equivalent to intensity.

Besides, those interested in literate societies are likely to enjoy certain distinct advantages over those dealing with nonliterate societies. Instead of having to count the houses and numbers of inhabitants, many students of literate societies can rely on published census reports or other records. Instead of having to sit for many sessions for one autobiography they are able to use ready-made autobiographies of notable men and women. Over and above all they are more likely to have available native social scientists for collaboration and their works for additional data and insights. Some linguists have already espressed the view that the quality of linguistic and semantic analyses can be greatly improved if native speakers are trained in the working techniques (Werner 1965:8–9). The works of many of our distinguished scholars on Japan, such as DeVos and Caudill, were done in collaboration with their Japanese counterparts. In other words, the possibly greater obstacles presented by the vastness or complexity of the literate societies than by nonliterate societies are at least compensated for by the possibly greater availability of published materials and indigenous assistance in the former than in the latter.

If, as we demonstrated before, there is an intrinsic relationship between the high and low traditions, between the center and the periphery, between the elite and the masses of literate societies, it seems that working on the high tradition, the center and the elite first—before we go to the low tradition, the periphery and the masses—will provide the anthropologist with great advantage in understanding the over-all design of the culture. The published material and the indigenous assistance may do just this.

The Reluctance To Study One's Own Culture

A third problem is the aversion on the part of some Western anthropologists to study their own cultures. As we noted previously, a few of them have tried their hands in this with good effect, but a majority have not touched it. Perhaps this aversion is related to what Kroeber once said:

> Quite likely our civilzation has its share of counterparts, which we cannot segregate off from the more practical remainder of the business of living because we are engulfed in this civilization of ours as we are in the air we breathe. Some centuries may be needed before the full recognition of our own non-rational couvades and totems and taboos become possible (1948:307).

The obvious answer to this is that if the Western anthropologists are too "engulfed" in their own particular civilizations to achieve relatively objective views of them, we should obviously train more non-Western anthropologists to scrutinize the "non-rational couvades and totems and taboos" in the Western ways of life rather than waiting for some centuries to come. In fact, the study of Western cultures by non-Western anthropologists is a methodological necessity.

More recently, the same aversion has been expressed in another way. In the latest edition of their book *An Introduction to Anthropology*, Beals and Hoijer make only the most brief mention of studies of literate societies under the subtitle "Modern Extensions of Anthropology" (1965:731–732) and they add this comment:

> Today the anthropologist, often in cooperation with other social scientists, has expanded his field to include the modern civilizations of Asia, Europe, and the Americas—cultures that in the anthropological sense are less well known than those of the American Indians or Stone Age man. . . .
> This extension of anthropological research, *though it has added little to theory*, has brought about a closer relationship between anthropology and sociology (1965: 731–732) (italics mine).

Our review thus far invalidates Beals and Hoijer's position that the many studies of literate societies have "added little to theory." Redfield's hypothesis of a link between the "Great Tradition" and the "Little Tradition," to be discussed later, and Foster's theory of the "Image of the Limited Good," which the Andersons find to be relevant to the aged in San Francisco, noted before, both emerged out of their studies of peasant villages in Latin America.

Beals and Hoijer have suffered on the theoretical level from their refusal to deal with studies of literate civilizations. This can be demonstrated with some precision. For example, in connection with religion they conclude:

> Religion functions importantly in reinforcing and maintaining cultural values. *Though few religions apparently are as explicitly linked to ethics and morality as, for example, Christianity and Judaism,* it is probably true that all or most religions tend, implicitly at least, to support and emphasize particular culturally defined standards of behavior (1965:599). (Italics mine.)

The last part of this quotation seems to be an obvious generality. To state "that all or most religions tend . . . to emphasize culturally defined standards of behavior" is no more than to say that "food tends to do something for all human bodies." The science of nutrition has progressed because the students have gone beyond that kind of generality and demonstrated what food does what to what aspect of the human body. Yet when Beals and Hoijer attempt to be somewhat more specific about what religions do for culture, in their more important part of the quotation, they are not very successful. Their statement suffers from unnecessary ethnocentrism, for there are religions in other societies quite as explicitly linked to ethics and morality as Christianity and Judaism. Far Eastern literate religions all fit that description, as does the Handsome Lake religion of the Iroquois (Wallace 1966a). It at once shows how the anthropological theory of religion can be defective because of the anthropologist's lack of concern with literate societies.

Patterns of Witch-Hunting: An Anthropological Misunderstanding

This defect may be documented in a variety of ways. Even confining ourselves to the field of religion, we can demonstrate how the anthropologist can well benefit in dealing with many problems by comparing data from nonliterate societies with those from literate societies. Only one of these can be considered here. This concerns the sharply contrasting ways of persecution and violence (even more than the theological ideas) connected with (or in the name of) some form of religion to be found in various societies. Take witchcraft and witch persecution, for example, which have been the subject of many papers, monographs, and books in general. To date there are at least three intensive anthropological inquiries (Evans-Pritchard 1937; Kluckhohn 1944; *Africa* 1935) and a number of shorter works (Cannon 1942; Nadel 1952; Krige 1947; LeVine

1962). The usual conclusions on witchcraft and witch hunting are that they are related to law and order, that witchcraft can have serious effect among people who believe in it, and that witch hunting is an outlet for psychological tensions. But such works remain partial analyses because none has highlighted the absolutistic attitude of the West toward witchcraft and witch hunting, as contrasted with the relativistic attitude of the rest of the world in this regard.

Witch hunting, as it occurred in Western countries, whether it be England, France, or Italy, had one outcome. Occasionally, the lives of some witches, confessed or alleged, might be spared, but more usually such persons were burned, hanged, drowned, or otherwise executed, because of their public offense. The estimates of scholars on the number of witches put to death in Europe vary enormously, from 30,000 to several million (Summers 1956:viii). Even if we take the lowest possible figure given here, however, there is no match for it among the more populous Asia or the rest of mankind. There was no way in Western societies for such persons to redeem themselves or to compensate their victims for their alleged wrongdoing as could be done elsewhere (Middleton and Winter 1963). Except for priests, who are part of the orthodoxy, no one could safely and openly resort to counterwitchcraft, for to possess counterwitchcraft would be maintaining traffic with devils and, hence, the victims themselves would be subject to accusation and persecution as witches (Kittredge 1929).

In contrast, witch hunting as it occurs in most or all non-Western societies usually has the following characteristics unknown in the West:

1. The lives of witches or sorcerers,[2] even after conviction, can be spared if the guilty ones or their kinsmen make compensation to the victims. Sometimes public confession of guilt on the part of the witches is enough. In other instances, the victims take action with only the intention of getting retribution payments. After confession and/or retribution, the guilty one will return to his or her former place in society without further difficulty.

2. There are always counterwitchcraft measures or white magic which are essentially the same sort of acts as those employed by the witches (alleged) or sorcerers (actual), but which are greatly valued by the people (Wolfe 1954). Possessors of such counterwitchcraft measures may even achieve positions of influence (Browne 1929; Firth 1954; and Hogbin 1934).

3. Where witches or sorcerers are reportedly "executed," they are more commonly put to death by angry private avengers related to the "victim" or by mob action. Even where there is a proper chieftainship with regular trial-conviction procedures, the penalty more usually befalls only those sorcerers who have killed by resorting to plain poison to aid their sorcery.

---

[2] In the Western world a difference has sometimes been made between witchcraft and sorcery. The former was generally associated with the intention of overthrowing the Christian belief, while the latter aimed at practices for personal ends only. There was, therefore, greater condemnation against the former than against the latter. An anthropologist made the distinction that sorcery consists of acts consciously practiced by the sorcerers with specific aims, while witchcraft results from actions of witches who may not even be aware of them (Nadel 1935). An examination of the pertinent literature fails to reveal any consistent distinction between these two terms (see Hsu 1960 for details).

It seems that in this absolutist-relativist difference lies a most fundamental aspect of the witch phenomena which is yet to be explored (Albert 1963a). A possible reply to the suggestion that we compare the witch phenomena in non-Western and Western societies is that witch hunting and witch belief are historical matters in the West, while in nonliterate societies they exist today; and that, in any case, such phenomena were "perversions" of true Christianity.

To this we must point out that, first, perversion should, by definition, occur only occasionally, but witch hunting and burning, like religious wars, occurred in the West with high frequency and over many centuries, with the full powers of the government behind them. When we speak of perversion of Christianity it is necessary to bear in mind that, from the Catholic point of view, the Protestant churches have long been regarded as perversion of the faith. In turn, from the Protestant point of view, the Mormon movement, the Amish faith, and even the Unitarian development are probably all perversions.

Furthermore, though not entirely clear, it does not seem unrealistic to link scapegoating, which remains a recurrent phenomenon, psychologically with witch belief. The substance has changed, the form has not. Witchcraft per se has receded from the top of Western culture, and it only exists as a "folk" belief in the periphery. But witch or witchlike fear expresses itself in the West openly and widely during many a crisis. During World War I it was the German minority who were designated the "Huns." In most of the post-World War I era the bearded, bomb-throwing Bolshevik took the place of the "Huns." In World War II it was the Japanese minority. During the period of the cold-war tensions the intellectual "Red" has been the object of persecution which only the Russian sputniks have helped to tone down. More recently, some sort of Chinese Communist agents have begun to replace the "Huns" of World War I, the Japanese of World War II, and the "Reds" of the United States-Russian cold-war days. Kittredge is on the right track when he says:

> That the belief in witchcraft is still pervasive among the peasantry of Europe, and to a considerable extent among the foreign-born population in this country, is a matter of common knowledge. Besides, spiritualism and kindred delusions have taken over, under changed names, many of the phenomena real or pretended, which would have been explained as due to witchcraft in days gone by . . . . The belief in witchcraft is the common heritage of humanity. It is not chargeable to any particular time, or race or form of religion (Kittredge 1929:370).

But he errs in not having perceived the basic difference in which the witch phenomenon is treated: the all-or-none, absolutist Western approach and the more-or-less relativist approach among the overwhelming majority of non-Western societies to witchcraft and witch hunting.

One can hardly blame Kittredge for this failure. As a traditional historian, he had no comparative tools, nor the intellectual interest, for delving into non-literate and Asian societies. He was merely dealing with the recurrence of the same phenomena in, as it were, two parts of the same cultural system, but it is surprising that no anthropological work on witchcraft thus far makes any explicit and systematic comparison. This is why a contrast of this magnitude has not figured in any anthropological theory on witch phenomena. The absolutist-relativist contrast is, in my view, fundamental to a sound understanding of religion in general, because in it we shall be able to find the root of why religion in the West has been linked with so much persecution, so many wars, separatist movements, and migrations (all of which are relevant to social and cultural development) as distinguished from the nonliterate and East Asian worlds.

Patterns of Religious Persecution and Cultural Development

How will the study of contrast between the West and the nonliterate and East Asian areas help in furthering our knowledge of human social and cultural development? The first thing to note is that the extent to which peoples persecute, or are willing to be persecuted, for religious reasons differs tremendously. The usual "scholarly" view is that religious persecution is universal. This view can be maintained by pointing, for example, to the Chinese persecution of Buddhists in the T'ang Dynasty and equating that uncritically with religious persecution in Europe (Yang 1961:122). This violates a fundamental rule of comparison which Boas enunciated more than half a century ago (1896). Briefly, his position was that the occurrence of the same phenomenon is not always due to the same causes (antecedental occurrences), and that legitimate comparison must be restricted to those phenomena which have been proved to be effects of the same causes. He went on to say:

> In researches on tribal societies those which have developed through association must be treated separately from those that have developed through disintegration. Geometrical designs which have arisen from conventionalized representations of natural objects must be treated separately from those that have arisen from technical motives. In short, before comparisons are made, the comparability of the material must be proved (Boas 1896:904).

We shall return to the problem of comparison later. In the present instance it should be noted once and for all that Chinese opposition to Buddhism in the T'ang Dynasty was very different from religious antagonisms in the West— Christians against Jews, Catholics against Protestants, and various kinds of Christians against diverse Fundamentalists, and such. The T'ang emperors did not regard Buddhism as an unmitigated evil so they did not attempt to eliminate it as a faith; they merely wished to make sure that the temples would not serve as hide-outs for rebels disguised as monks and nuns.

The T'ang government's "persecutory" actions were in accord with these ideas. First, it required all monks and nuns to be registered and regulated to make sure they were bona-fide religious functionaries. Second, it stipulated that "only two temples with thirty monks each were permitted to stand in each of the two capitals, Changan and Loyang. Of the 228 prefectures in the Empire, only the capital cities of the 'first grade' prefectures were permitted to retain one temple each with ten monks" (Hu 1953:17). Third, temples in excess of the authorized number were destroyed, while monks and nuns in excess of the authorized number were forced to revert to civilian life. As a result, thousands of temples were destroyed and nearly a quarter of a million monks and nuns left the temples.

Several points of Chinese-Western contrast in these acts of Chinese religious persecution are worth noting. For one thing, in contrast to the West, the T'ang authorities did not attempt to stamp out Buddhism by executing the Buddhists or by inquisition to root out lingering Buddhist faith or practices among those who had publicly repudiated it. For another, in contrast to the West, there were no Chinese mob attacks against Buddhists or mass revivals of other faiths to compete for the stray souls. Finally, in contrast to the West, Chinese persecution of Buddhism was short-lived, limited to four occurrences between about 700 and 955 A.D. and completely disappeared after the latter date.

The significance of these contrasts for the respective Western and Chinese social and cultural developments remains to be clearly ascertained by future researches, but is not hard to perceive even without massive documentation. For example, the relativistic approach of the T'ang emperors in religious persecution was matched by a similar response on the part of the monks and nuns forced to leave the temples and monasteries, for none of the latter resisted the order. The authorities got their wishes without having to resort to execution or imprisonment. It is difficult to find or envisage a similar course of events in the entire religious history of the West, where men have gone to the stake for much less than was required of these T'ang monks and nuns.

The usual emphasis in any modern-day study of religious persecution (especially that of the past) is on the persecutors—that there were bad people bent on victimizing believers. It is not generally realized that, except in a situation like that of Nazi Germany where all Jews were to be eliminated, in order to have a good religious persecution there must not only exist would-be persecutors but also people who regard their religion as more important than their lives. The Chinese emperors did not entertain the extreme position of complete extermination; and the Chinese Buddhist lacked the commitment to resist at any price.

The consequence of this Chinese approach was not only that religious persecution was short-lived but that there arose no need for Chinese Buddhists to go underground, to form protestant or reformist movements, to emigrate en masse, or to ally themselves with some non-Chinese invaders. Above all, the remaining monks and nuns came to a sort of rapprochement with the political power and adjusted themselves to Chinese cultural demands without further struggle. For example, the hallmark of monkhood was the severance of all kinship relations and obligations, including the worship of ancestors. One major complaint of the Chinese literati against monkhood was that, since they did not marry they would not have descendants to look after their needs and therefore their souls were liable to become vagabond ghosts giving trouble to other normal ancestral spirits. So most Chinese Buddhist monasteries, in contrast to their counterparts elsewhere, each had as a rule an "ancestral" altar for all of its deceased inmates.

---

[3] Which understandably may be derogatorily called the wishy-washy approach by those who will not accept anything short of complete victory.

This "moderation" approach to religion[3] was not only incompatible with that of early Christians in Europe but is also not palatable to their modern descendants in the United States. It was certainly unacceptable to Western missionaries, who went to convert the Middle Kingdom to the Lord, but the Chinese approach to Christianity could not significantly differ from their approach to Buddhism. Finding their approach to religion incompatible with that of Christian missionaries, only less than 1 percent of the Chinese ever embraced Christianity. It is due to this fact and to the fact that the Chinese approach is shared by a majority of Asians, including the Japanese, and by most Africans, and not to the true geographical origin of Christianity, that Christianity came to be known in the world today as a Western religion. For not only nearly all Western men became Christian, but practically all the Christian missionaries of the world are still of Western origin. One cannot expect nonliterate societies with relatively low levels of organization and little social stratification to send out missionaries. One could certainly have expected the Chinese to do so, but they did not.

Given the Chinese (and in this regard the East Asian and African as well) approach, changes in religion tend to be small and mild, for new creeds and cults are likely to be simply added to the old; but given the Western approach, changes in religion tend to be large and explosive, for even minor revisions of the old are likely to be claimed as totally new and, therefore, the upholders of that claim will seem to force a complete replacement of the old. Even if they do not actually back up their claims by acts, such claims cannot but arouse anxiety on the part of others. It encourages those in support of the new to be militant and those for the old to be extremely defensive. The tremendous consequences that this differential approach to religion has made in the world of man can never be reflected in anthropological theory concerning religion so long as we sweep aside anthropological studies of literate societies.[4]

---

[4] The differences between Western and Chinese approaches to religion are more fully treated in Hsu (1955:235–277). The unfortunate theoretical consequences of the anthropologist's failure to study his own culture have been discussed in Hsu (1967a).

7

Some Guiding Principles

S O FAR WE HAVE DEALT with the more negative aspects of the problems in
the study of literate societies. Now we must see what can be done to improve the art and science of studying literate civilizations.

Cultural Similarities versus Cultural Differences

First, there is a need to settle the unnecessary quarrel between those who
emphasize universals among cultures and others who concentrate on their differences. The study of universals is legitimate and it can be done on many levels.
If Géza Róheim's followers wish to concentrate on the unity of mankind through
ascertaining the similarity in their patterns of the unconscious, this is a perfectly
legitimate scientific pursuit, provided that they follow some basic rules of science
and do not engage in free association. Similarly, if Murdock wants to emphasize
the "common denominator of cultures" (1945) and students of Kluckhohn wish
to refine his "universal categories of culture" (1962), these are also scientifically
laudable tasks.

In a more restricted sense we can attempt to establish universals in religion (Wallace 1966b), in the maintenance of law and order, in art, and such, but
the study of universals should not negate and certainly is not in conflict with the
study of differences among societies and cultures. Peoples reared in different
societies with different cultural traditions do as a whole behave differently in many
major and minor ways, and such differences in behavior are ascertainable, consistent, and important. American businessmen inevitably find that their Japanese
counterparts negotiate with them differently. Englishmen frequently find the
Hindu way in religion exasperating.

We can fully agree with Róheim's observation that peasant families the
world over exhibit many similarities:

40

The family is a working unit, children are not educated according to pedagogical principles. There is hardly any difference between what adults eat and what children eat after they are weaned. A child of five is not a human being who is different from an adult, he is just a small adult. Education does not take place systematically, the child gradually "grows into" (belenö) the behavior pattern of the adult. He takes care of small domestic animals while the parents take care of the larger ones. Children's play is an imitation of adult work (1950:391).

We cannot, however, agree with him that "it is rather the nature of the peasant to run away from absolutely unbearable circumstances, that is, to emigrate as in the past, to Poland or Moldavia, and recently to America" (1950:391). This may be true of Polish peasants or New England Yankees (Homans 1950:454), but not of their Chinese brethren. Chinese peasants have been known to be noticeably reluctant to emigrate even from one region of the country to another, and if they were forced to emigrate, they maintained a very strong tie with their home area and would generally want to be buried there if they should die elsewhere (Hsu 1963:145–147).

The study of cultural universals and that of cultural differences are two separate undertakings on different levels of abstraction. They should not be confounded with each other. Over and above their cultural universals (or in spite of them), different peoples do react to similar problems (whether they originate in human relationships or environmental conditions) in very dissimilar ways and seek widely different solutions to them.

Without denigrating the importance of cultural universals, I am of the opinion that the systematic exploration of cultural differences must occupy a central place in anthropology for years to come. These differences are the foundation on which our science is built and grows, whether we hope to tackle the problem of culture change or evolution, interaction between cultures, transmission and diffusion of cultures, the relationship between culture and human development, or taxonomy of cultures.

Delineating the Culture Pattern

One approach unique to anthropology is the study of societies and cultures as wholes. Can we expect to achieve this goal when we deal with large literate societies and cultures? I believe that we can and must strive to arrive at an over-all culture pattern of each literate society, in spite of its size and complexity, just as we try to achieve overviews of many a nonliterate society, but to do this effectively we need hypotheses about cultures, literate as well as nonliterate, at a structural level, not crude predictions at a phenomenal level.

It is not that we must caricature any culture; the need to arrive at an over-all picture is based on the fundamental assumption in modern anthropology of social and cultural integration. Previously, we already noted that all societies, literate and nonliterate, tend to present internal variability to a degree, and that insufficient attention has been paid to this fact by most anthropologists. But even if the heterogeneity of a society is so pronounced that it may be designated a "plural" society, there will still be unity on some level.[1] Each society is a more or less organized whole unless there is an active revolution which threatens to pull it asunder. The way of life of each society tends more or less to be coherent, continuous, and distinctive when contrasted with that of another.

This concept of integration was rooted in functionalism, usually attributed to Malinowski, which was a principal antidote against diffusionism, the anthropological fashion of his day. Diffusionists, because they were not interested in integration saw cultural traits and artifacts flowing from one society to another whenever human groups came into contact. But functionalism and its later concept of integration added a dimension by stipulating that societies and cultures will accept only those elements or artifacts which fit or in some way articulate with a previously existing pattern.

The enormous size and complexity of some literate societies would, of course, make the task of arriving at over-all structural patterns difficult, but not impossible. The obvious difference between literate and nonliterate societies is the presence or absence of written languages. What has not been generally realized is, however, the true bearing of written languages on the development of cultures and societies.

In an earlier publication (1961b) I pointed out the fact that no native African tribes south of the Sahara had a written language, even though at one time or another they came into contact with either the Egyptian hieroglyphics or the Indo-European alphabets.[2] My inference is that the creation of a written

---

[1] Despres attempts to perfect a methodology which will enable us to distinguish homogeneous societies, each containing no significant cultural and linguistic differences; heterogeneous ones, each containing "local cultural sections," which are not reflected on the national level through separate institutional structures; and pluralistic ones, each containing national institutional structures which maintain the cultural differentiations of the various locally integrated groups (Despres 1966), but I think these categories must be seen as forming a continuum. For example, the United States is more heterogeneous than Japan because it contains many more local ethnic groups than the latter, but less pluralistic than Belgium, where Flemish and French speeches are used in the national legislatures and where schools are separate. The contrast between Belgium and Canada, however, is not so clear. Both may have to be considered "plural," though they are different in obvious ways. Similarly, there are considerable differences between the ways of the minorities in the United States and those of, for example, the Bretons in France, though both must be considered more heterogeneous than plural.

[2] Amharic, of Ethiopia and Tanarec, of a Berber tribe, are the only two written languages in North Africa besides the Egyptian hieroglyphics. The latter was replaced by Arabic with the coming of Islam. The prehistoric Mereoitic-speaking people in northern Sudan (bordering Egypt) probably used a form of Egyptian hieroglyphics, but this is not yet entirely deciphered. The history of the Kanuri of Nigeria is known through documents written by Kanuri religious leaders or Mallams, who knew and used Arabic, which is the language of law and was, until 1900 A.D., the language of diplomacy in the Sudan and North Africa. The oldest Kanuri document extant is written in Arabic by a Kanuri named Ahmed ibn Fartua: *History of the First Twelve Years of the Reign of Mai Idris Alooma of Bornu* (1571–1583), translated from the Arabic with Introduction and Notes by H. R. Palmer (1926). The Kanuri did invent an alphabet, but somehow this was not used. I am indebted to Ronald Cohen for the Kanuri information.

The Vai people of northwest Liberia also created a syllabary of their own in the early nineteenth century, but it never gained circulation and is not known at present. Probably

language (with borrowed elements or otherwise) and its continued use depends upon the presence of a strong need for a wide circle of communication and for a lasting preservation of the relationships with the past, besides requiring a concerted and continuous group exertion (Hsu 1961b:444).

I now wish to observe that the consequences in social and cultural development of the use of written languages must also have been considerable for many peoples. With written languages came longer histories, greater accumulations from the past in the ideational as well as material level, greater specialization, more periods of efflorescence in which those who had more leisure than others could reflect on fancy problems and views of man, his world, and his destiny.

All of these tend to culminate in one fundamental characteristic, on the structural level, of literate civilizations as contrasted with nonliterate cultures: the possibility of greater abstraction. For evidence of this fact we do not even have to go to historical China or India or Europe and point to their high philosophies or theologies. The contemporary United States can serve as an equally good example.

There is, for example, the present-day American tendency to stress the desirability of the natural and the direct in many things: miniskirts, handmade wares, LSD,[3] modern art, naturalistic modern dancing, beatniks, sex education,[4] Dr. Spock, nudist colonies, church rituals in English, and a house in the woods. The inventory is endless. In other and more fundamental aspects, however, life has become less natural, less direct, and, therefore, more complicated as well as more abstract, as apparent in national aims and behavior, economic vicissitudes, personality trends, theological developments, legislative and judicial tendencies, computerization of life symbolized by zip codes and social security numbers, and changes in the relationship between organization and the individual. The inventory is equally endless.

The trend toward greater abstraction is not due simply to the greater complexity of literate civilizations compared to their nonliterate counterparts. The fact is that many aspects of the American civilization do stress the "natural" (and, in fact, become more "natural" and cater more to the individual needs and whims) in spite of the growing complexity of the society as a whole. In contrast, in spite of the search for the "natural," many aspects of the American civilization become not only less clear and understandable to the individual but also seem to be more and more out of his control. The latter trend is not recent. Its central place in American civilization is still encapsulated in such mysteries as the

---

such an invention occurred several times through the efforts of enterprising individuals in sub-Sahara, but was lost because of the lack of general support.

In the New World Afaka, a Djuka (Aucan Bush Negro) in Dutch Giana invented a syllabary around 1900 which was used by Catholic missionaries to produce a series of booklets containing the major Catholic prayers and dogma. The script contains fifty-six syllabaries. It never became popular among the Bush Negroes and is possibly not used at all today. I am indebted to Dirk van der Elst for the information on Afaka's script.

[3] Defended by its users and promoters as "a kind of lens through which they see more clearly, more beautifully", for "it makes things look like they really are" (*Life* 1967).

[4] In a recent TV program (1968) an M.D. proposed that children should be given the opportunity to witness the sexual act between their parents as part of their sex education.

Creation and the Immaculate Conception which, despite paleontological discoveries and sex education, have not been touched. Other literate civilizations possess, of course, different kinds of mysteries and characteristic abstractions.

To understand literate civilizations of such magnitude we must aim at more abstraction on a higher level rather than rely on the head-counting, down-to-earth type of study that we use with nonliterate cultures. For this reason I cannot agree with those who maintain that, by introducing such a label as "plural society" and insisting on more elaborate techniques of field investigation, they will successfully and simply extend more traditional, small-scale studies to much more complex phenomena (Despres 1966).

A striking illustration of the pitfalls of attempting to study a large literate civilization with myopic tools is found in the sharp contrast between Ruth Benedict's study of Japan at a distance and Jean Stoetzel's later work on the same country with more research money, more assistants, more tests, and more on-the-spot observation and interview. A host of criticisms, both Japanese and Western, have been leveled against Ruth Bendedict's *The Chrysanthemum and the Sword* (1946). While American critics, especially those "against" patterns, often regarded Benedict's work as being overly sweeping and, therefore, oversimplified, her Japanese critics have concentrated on six major issues of methodology.

1. Her use of the term "Japanese" needs more precise definition. Did she refer to the man in the street, to all Japanese, to the military and fascist cliques during World War II, or to the ideal typical Japenese?

2. The meaning of the word "culture" possesses certain ambiguities. How does this "design for living" of a society fit in with the "institutional heterogeneity" of Japanese society?

3. She used "empirical data" from one period of time (for example, the Tokugawa period) to draw generalizations about behavior in another (for example, the present time).

4. There is a "need for an 'institutional' approach" to supplement Benedict's "whole-cultural approach."

5. There is the necessity to recognize that "the problem of historical change" through which some features of Japanese values may "appear archaic to the outsider, and may, indeed, have a considerable historical depth, but they may be in actuality existing in form only, and quite changed in function. The culture may thus sometimes resemble, in formal aspect, a patchwork of elements of many different ages, and one cannot predict or understand the whole merely from a knowledge of one of the pieces."

6. Benedict did not have an interdisciplinary team which could make her understanding of Japanese society more comprehensive.[5]

However, though some of these criticisms are valid, they do not necessarily insure a better way of doing what Benedict did. Jean Stoetzel met many of the

---

[5] A comprehensive summary of these Japanese criticisms is found in Bennett and Nagai 1953.

methodological structures by going into the field with a team and fancy investigatory devices. Unfortunately, he was without insight or theoretical preparation for the necessary abstraction. The result is his much inferior book *Without the Chrysanthemum and Sword* (1955). The conditions under which the latter piece of research was done could not be more different than those under which Benedict did hers. Benedict never went to Japan and her sources of data were published materials and Japanese informants in the United States. Stoetzel, a French sociologist, assisted by a Dutch scholar named Vos, who knew the Japanese language well, went to Japan for three or four months in 1951–1952. Stoetzel made use of a battery of tests administered in five geographical locations as disparate as Kagoshima in southern Kyushu, Kyoto and Tokyo, Sapporo and Nemuro in Hokkaido. The tests used included a modified version of that TAT by Sofue and the Allport-Gillespie test. Several different questionnaires were administered in different areas, and eight autobiographies were collected. In addition, Stoetzel and Vos had the help of public opinion polls taken by the National Public Opinion Research Institute of Japan and an intensive seminar under the auspices of the Japanese Association of Cultural Science.

What Stoetzel has given us is rich in sociological meandering, but extremely poor as an aid in understanding Japan and her way of life, even restricted to the attitudes of youth in postwar Japan, on which he and his assistant Vos concentrated. Their conclusions are no more than a summary of what their questionnaires or test results appeared to reveal. They see that the "behavior patterns of young Japanese exhibit not only a fair amount of inexperience but also much vacillation." They find that the Japanese youth exhibits utilitarian tendencies more than any other. They also find evidence for an "unmistakable interest" in "cultural values" because a considerable percentage of them say that "if they unexpectedly received a large sum of money" they would spend it on study or buying books. The Japanese youth appears to be ambitious and optimistic, which is said to be in accord with the two previous findings, but the Japanese youth also gives evidence of "passiveness, insecurity, and escapism," which is in contradiction to what had been seen before. Finally, the Japanese youth also desires dependence on others. From this conglomeration of evidence, Stoetzel says that "the most obvious conclusion to be drawn from this attempted analysis of the personality of young Japanese is their immaturity" (1955:201–237).

Quite apart from the fact that we cannot easily agree that the Japanese youth's need for personal dependence or passiveness is a sign of immaturity, Stoetzel has given us no real interpretation of either the conflicting data coming from the actual investigation or the meaning of what he finds about Japanese youth in terms of the Japanese pattern of life as a whole. When one has finished the book, one is face to face with the inevitable conclusion that many investigatory devices have been used and certain results have been produced by those efforts, but these devices and results provide us with no clear delineation of the patterns of Japanese society and culture in support, refutation, or revision of what Benedict has given us. Benedict's work remains the masterpiece on Japanese national character, yet to be challenged.

We are in need of over-all patterns for given societies to serve as points of reference against which the different aspects or elements of that culture may be examined, but we cannot find a pattern in Stoetzel's book in spite of his team of collaborators and his battery of methodological devices. Stoetzel's failure either to remedy the alleged deficiencies of Benedict's work or to match its scientific brilliance highlights the fact that attempts at coverage by greater accumulation of data from different regions and different sections of the population do not necessarily carry us far. An anthropological study is different from a sociological survey. In this regard Margaret Mead correctly expresses the anthropological position:

Anthropological sampling is not a poor and inadequate version of sociological or socio-psychological sampling, a version where *n* equals too few cases. *It is simply a different kind of sampling*, in which the validity of the sample depends not so much upon the number of cases as upon the proper specification of the informant, so that he or she can be accurately placed, in terms of a very large number of variables—age, sex, order of birth, family background, life-experience, temperamental tendencies (such as optimism, habit of exaggeration, etc.), political and religious position, exact situational relationship to the investigator, configurational relationship to every other informant, and so forth. Within this very extensive degree of specification, each informant is studied as a perfect example, an organic representation of his complete cultural experience. This . . . is comparable to the elaboration with which the trained historian specifies the place of a crucial document among the few and valuable documents available for a particular period, or experiments in medicine in which a large number of measurements are made on a small number of cases.

The second misunderstanding centers around a differential interest in pattern. The sociologist or social psychologist who questions the anthropologist by saying, "But you don't know what the distribution of resistance to paternal authority is," is interested in *how much* of measurable quantities of an entity called "resistance to paternal authority" can be found to be distributed in the total population. But the anthropologist is interested in the *pattern* of resistances and respect, neutralities and intensities, in regard to parents and grandparents and siblings, and the way in which this pattern can be found in other sets of relationships between employer and employee, writer and reader, and so on. The difference in emphasis may be illustrated from linguistics: if one wants to know the grammatical structure of a language, it is sufficient to use very few informants about whom the necessary specified information has been collected; if one wants to know how many people use a certain locution or a particular word in preference to another, then sampling of the wider type is necessary, although probably not sufficient . . . . In dealing with culture, the anthropologist makes the same assumptions about the rest of a culture that the linguist makes about the language—that he is dealing with a system which can be delineated by analysis of a small number of very highly specified samples. The decision as to *how many* informants are needed is primarily a structural decision . . . . The transformation of the statement, "In American culture the dwelling house has opaque walls," into quantitative statements about how many Americans live in such houses—about how many members of a society act *directly* in terms of a cultural stereotype—actually makes it a statement of a different order. All the members of a society may recognize that the correct form of marriage is for a man to marry his mother's father's mother's father's sister's son's daughter's son's daughter, but actually no such marriage may exist at the moment of observation. The determination of the prevalence and incidence of any piece of behavior requires detailed observation of a large sample of individuals, in primitive societies by studying the entire community, in large complex societies by using elaborate sampling methods of the sociological sort (Mead 1962:408–410).[6]

If some anthropologists (and other social scientists as well) prefer merely to determine the prevalence and incidence of any item of behavior, that is their privilege. However, we must note that, in that case, even detailed observation of a large sample of the separate items will not give us an adequate idea of the whole. I would go one step further than Mead in this regard. In my view the anthropologist must not stop at the statement: "In American culture the dwelling house has opaque walls." (Mead's example.) He must also attempt to ascertain the bearing of the opaque walls of the dwelling house on the American pattern of family relationship, on American class status symbolism, and so forth—in other words, the place of the opaque walls of the American dwelling house in the larger context of American society and culture.

Some anthropologists may, of course, argue that an over-all pattern is not always possible because not all aspects in every society, especially at the ideational level, are perfectly integrated. Some mature American anthropologists may find, for example, the "teenys" on Sunset Boulevard much more alien to their belief system and way of life than the Blood Indians. Others may find Pop and Op arts difficult to reconcile with classical Western art history, or see militants and pacifists or racists and believers of equality as total opposites in the same society. Such facts have led some observers to the conclusion that American culture is characterized by irreconcilables, but even these are not so alien to each other when we raise our level of abstraction and view them in terms of the larger Western social and cultural context, a context in which protests against orthodoxy or tradition and separatist movements have always been part and parcel of its nature (Hsu 1961a, 1963:192–231; Albert 1963a:28). These are characteristics of a society and civilization in which change enjoys a high premium (though the idea of change is constant), as distinguished from others in which the traditional ways hold strong and attacks on them spring chiefly from strong external pressure or threat.

Providing Social and Cultural Context
for the Village Study

Third, having said that we need higher levels of abstraction in dealing with literate civilizations than with nonliterate ones, we must then find relatively specific methodological procedures for relating localized details to their large social and cultural contexts. Earlier in this book I already pointed out the basic difference between a nonliterate tribe and a village in a literate society, but even apart from the fact that a village in a literate society is less likely to be isolated, there are other imperative reasons for this need. Whether the anthropologist likes it or not, he will, even if he has done only as much as one village study in India or

---

[6] Quoted from *Anthropology Today: Selections* edited by Sol Tax. By permission of Margaret Mead and The University of Chicago Press.

Japan or Indonesia, be called upon to teach courses on "Indian Culture," "Japanese Family," "Indonesian Village Life," "Japanese Political Institutions," and so forth, or, from time to time, either for scientific or practical reasons, be forced to react to any of these civilizations as a whole. Is it not a matter of scientific and pedagogic necessity for such scholars to become a little better prepared by looking into the connections between their own villages and the wider civilization as a whole?

In fact, there will be strong temptations at all times for any scholar investigating a single village to extend his generalizations to the larger literate society, for the simple reason that many of the facts pertaining to the larger literate society cannot help but come to his attention even when he tries to avoid them. For example, any scholar working on China or India is likely to have known something about Chinese history or Indian art through writings by nonanthropologists. The anthropologist himself, or some other scholar, will see obvious congruences, but especially divergences, between what he has found in one village and what is already known about the larger society. The anthropologist himself will feel the need to explain these, or other people will force him to do so. The anthropologist dealing with literate civilizations simply cannot confine himself to one village. He may surely do fieldwork in one village, but he must look for ways to relate his village to the larger national whole.

One way of relating the village study to the over-all literate civilization of which it forms a part is to employ the idea of continuous interaction between a "great tradition," as abstracted and systematized by the specialist literati, mainly in urban centers, and the "little traditions" of village communities, as first expressly stated by Redfield (Redfield and Singer 1952; Redfield 1955). This idea has been considerably refined and operationalized in connection with the study of India by Marriott, Singer, and associates (Marriott 1955). In the Hindu society three main processes in the interaction between the great tradition and the little tradition are distinguishable: sanskritization, parochialization, and universalization. Sanskritization is the process whereby a low caste has adopted the customs, rites, and beliefs of the higher caste Brahmans in order to rise to a higher position. Parochialization supplements the process of Sanskritization. It refers to the fact that in its downward spread, the great tradition is obstructed or transformed by the indigenous little tradition. Universalization is the process whereby the materials of a little tradition are carried forward to form a relatively more articulate and refined indigenous civilization (Srinivas 1952:30, 1955–1956:492–496; Marriott 1955:197–201).

The works of Redfield, Singer, and Marriott are aimed at clarifying the processes according to which elements from the local areas and the larger civilization flow or influence each other. A different way of getting at the relationship between the village and the larger society is to be found in Hoebel's idea of postulates formulated in connection with his study of "primitive" law.

Once a culture gets under way (and all the cultures with which social science has to deal *are* under way) there are always some criteria of choice that govern or influence selection. These criteria are the broadly generalized propositions held by the members of a society as to the nature of things and as to what is qualitatively desirable and undesirable. We prefer to call these basic propositions "postulates." (Hoebel 1954: 13).

Although Hoebel is dealing only with law in nonliterate societies (Eskimo, Ifugao, Comanche, Kiowa, Cheyenne, Trobriand Islander, Ashanti),[7] his concept of postulates can be applied with great profit to linking villages with their larger society. If we find the assumptions and choices behind the customs in the smaller community to be commensurate with, or converging in the direction of, those underlying the law of the larger society, we then shall have reasonable ground to suppose a close cultural link between the two. We shall return to Hoebel's postulates later.

Smith and Reyes speak of the importance of similar links between a Japanese agricultural community and the larger Japanese social and cultural context. Their conclusions are worth quoting:

> Opler has suggested that the unity and identity of a community are a part of the same process as its extensions. Our material sustains this view and suggests that if we are to understand those "areas and periods of common life of more or less intensity" which we call communities, systematic attention must be given the nature and pattern of the interrelations of such units with the world around them. The data further suggest that community contacts do not necessarily result in deculturation or even significant acculturation for rural or other types of relatively isolated communities. On the other hand, it is clear that change at the community level cannot be understood without an understanding of the role of agencies outside the community, for it is our impression that purely internal change unrelated to outside factors is a relatively rare phenomenon. How meaningless, then, to discuss community change as though outside forces only incidentally impinge. Only after we have mapped out the network of interrelations within which it operates can we begin to understand the internal functioning of a given community (Smith and Reyes 1957:471).

My work on India, China, the United States, and Japan (Hsu 1955, 1963, 1968b) is especially predicated on the general notion that in studying literate civilizations one can no more confine oneself to a village or local phenomenon than to the high scriptures and philosophies. The investigation is concentrated neither exclusively on the high ideal nor exclusively on the localized reality of any particular time and place, but on the interaction between local and national (as well as between reality and ideal) and on the significance of both in terms of the whole. The sacred books and most of the literary creations such as myths, folktales, dramas, novels, and the like, probably express aspects of the ideal of each society more than its reality. The contemporary facts garnered in different parts of the country, either by the sociological technique of topical inquiry or by the anthropological technique of community study, naturally approximate its reality more than its ideal. It has also been my deliberate procedure to ignore the time differences between the literary, artistic, folkloristic, and other written time materials and the sociological facts observed by my colleagues and myself, and to concentrate on the relationship between the two.

---

[7] In his book *The Cheyennes: Indians of the Great Plains* Hoebel applied the postulate method to the entire Cheyenne culture in general (1960:98–99).

Some students of folklore or history may be interested, for example, in which gods or goddesses worshipped today are survivals of which gods or goddesses in the ancient lores, or in the marriage of Draupadi to the five Pandava brothers reported in the epic Mahabharata, as origin of tribal polyandry in India. Some students of caste are interested in tracing how the Gujara group, through a continuous process of spread and absorption, came to include diverse castes of different statuses (from Kshatriyas to near Untouchables) and in diverse localities (from Maharashtra to Delhi to Punjab), none of which may be aware of any or all of the others (Karve 1961:62–65), but the student of the science of culture must be primarily oriented toward the comparison of data, wherever they are found, in terms of the similarity or differences in underlying patterns or ideas. In their summary of and comment on Bougle's and Hocart's theories on caste, Dumont and Pocock define the position succinctly: "Here [meaning their studies] texts are used not as historical evidence with which it is presumed that the present must accord but rather as offering certain systems of ideas with which the present may be compared" (Dumont and Pocock 1958:49).

It is the relationship between the structural patterns revealed by the texts or historical data and those discernible in the present events which will help us to understand every society, unless we assume little or no integrative process in each social system. For example, before the reader succumbs to the feeling that the Hindu sacred books have little connection with the life of the common people, he should reflect for a moment on the following fact in Western society. The actual behavior of the nominally Christian peoples may not be very "Christian," but there are few scholars or laymen who will insist that the Bible and other religious writings emanating from it have no bearing to the common people born in Christianity. Illiteracy on the part of the common people of India has been no bar to knowledge of the ancient heritage. The Vedas and other sacred literature are constantly recited and explained by traveling kathaks (storytellers) and holy men all over India, while the epics are dramatized and told in a thousand ways to all types of audiences. Of course, neither set of data is to be considered primary in the ultimate sense, but each influences the other.

Likewise, the Confucian precepts in China were certainly not all original creations of the sage himself. Some of the mores and customs he endorsed and propounded must have existed long before him in some parts of China, but after his teachings were widely known they, in turn, affected and reshaped the mores and customs of the Chinese as a whole. This process is essentially similar to what folklorists describe as "circular flow," which requires "time to simmer," "to integrate," "to rework" (Foster 1953:164).

Ahistorical Treatment of Historical Data

From the same methodological standpoint, sequences of facts and events—from historical to modern—can also be compared in an ahistorical but analytic frame of reference based on the facts of development. The numerous characteristics which distinguish one biological organism from another are usually absent in early life. In fact, the embryos of frogs and human beings in their earliest stages look remarkably similar. At birth the differences between a human being and a chimpanzee also appear negligible. The emergence of physical or behavioral characteristics which distinguish some biological organisms from others requires, in some instances, a few months and, in other instances, many years. Hence, a science of living things must be based on the characteristics of adults, although those of infants are also of interest. The characteristics which distinguish one society from another develop as a result of interaction among forces within the same society or as a result of mutual pressures between different societies. Sometimes these characteristics emerge quickly, but more often they do not do so for a long time—not infrequently centuries. The French Revolution cannot be understood sociologically if we study only the facts pertaining to the reign of Louis XVI, for the simple reason that it was not only related to a wider European development which sprang from seeds sown in the reign of Louis XIV and earlier, but also to the Magna Carta, the Enlightenment philosophies, the industrial revolution, and so forth. In turn, the forces underlying the French Revolution had a great deal to do with the American Revolution, the Chinese revolutions, the Meiji Restoration of Japan, and so on.

It is, therefore, methodologically sound to find connections between the French Revolution and the signing of the Magna Carta, even though the two events occurred nearly six centuries apart, and to relate the American Revolution to the Chinese and Japanese developments, even though they occurred at different times and on different continents. It is for this reason that social scientists can speak of the repetitive social or cultural process, for processes which are repetitive through time are not the specific events and personalities but the patterns and ideas behind the events, or the roles and thought patterns molding or motivating the individuals.

The same methodological considerations govern my efforts to relate more or less contemporaneous facts from different geographical sections of India, China, the United States, or Japan. The repeated emergence of some form of protestant movements in Hinduism, and the repeated incorporation of such movements into the same Hinduism through its caste framework, are characteristic Indian phenomena of long standing. The examples range from Jainism which began nearly two thousand years ago to Bhaktism, just a few centuries back. In modern times, however, the Vedanta movement, which instituted schools, public forums, and boys' clubs and dispatched missionaries abroad must be seen as at least partially due to Western influence. Therefore, it may be profitably studied in conjunction with Japanese efforts to spread state Shintoism to Korea, Marianas, and, later, Manchuria at the height of Japanese military power before and during World War II, which must also be linked with the impact of the West.

The difference between the Indian Vedanta movement and the spread of Japanese Shintoism is no less significant. While both cultures were reacting to Western pressures, the Indian development remained a private matter, but the Japanese development was an arm of the political state. Each culture reacted to external influences in characteristic ways of its own.

We already noted earlier in this book how Chinese persecution of Buddhism in the sixth and seventh centuries was liable to misinterpretation, expecially if we fail to see the fact that it was a short-lived phenomenon in Chinese history. The pattern of race relations (especially Negro-white relations) in the United States, however, cannot be gauged merely from the origin of slavery, plantations, the Civil War, and states' rights. It must also be examined in terms of the pressures for desegregation of schools and residences and of the civil rights movement in general, which since World War II has received special impetus from America's involvements vis-à-vis Africa. In particular, the fact that some American Negroes seek a degree of African identity cannot be understood without knowledge of the rise of native African states in post-World War II years.

The Comparative Approach (Contrasted with Cross-cultural Studies)

Finally, we need to study all cultures and civilizations in a comparative framework. The comparative approach has often been aired as a possibility, but has so far not been clearly and comprehensively understood. It is sometimes confused with cross-cultural studies and interdisciplinary studies. The analysis of juvenile delinquency in Chicago by a psychiatrist and a sociologist is interdisciplinary but not cross-cultural or comparative. Cross-cultural studies are only one variety of comparative studies. They are works involving a few variables in a large number of societies employing statistical techniques. Thus, Hobhouse, Wheeler, and Ginsberg's *The Material Culture and Social Institutions of Simpler Peoples* (1915), Murdock's *Social Structure* (1949), Whiting and Child's *Child Training and Personality* (1953), Homans and Schneider's *Marriage, Authority and Final Causes* (1955), Cohen's "Food and Its Vicissitudes: A Cross-Cultural Study of Sharing and Non-Sharing" (1961) are examples of cross-cultural studies; but Benedict's *Patterns of Culture* (1934), Mead's *Competition and Cooperation Among Primitive Peoples* (1937), Bohannan's *African Homicide and Suicide* (1960), and my books *Americans and Chinese: Two Ways of Life* (1955) and *Clan, Caste and Club* (1963) better serve as examples of comparisons in depth rather than cross-cultural studies. They each deal with a few societies as wholes or selected aspects of each society in terms of how the aspects fit in with each whole. If we deal with a large number of societies, the number of variables that we can scrutinize is bound to be small, while if we deal with only a few societies, we shall be in a position to look at more of these variables.

Whether we concern ourselves with many or a few societies, a comparative framework is indispensable to the development of anthropology.

Although the cross-cultural type of comparison was envisaged by one of the earliest anthropologists, Tylor, the main body of anthropological works is composed of studies each concentrated on one single people. This is the typical ethnography. In this way we have developed among anthropologists expressions such as "your tribe," "my tribe," or "this is not true of my tribe." Ethnographies are almost always works on single societies.[8]

Quite apart from the fact that the theories making for a science of man cannot each be developed out of single instances, there are two basic reasons why this single-society approach is inadequate. First, even the works on a single society usually imply some sort of "comparison," if not with other nonliterate societies, at least with the societies from which the anthropologists have come. Furthermore, even anthropologists who did no work on literate civilization (and expressly eschew it) have at one point or another broken their resolve and made cursory or implicit comparisons or contrasts between the so-called primitive and "our own" (which can mean American, French, English, Hungarian, or "Western" as a whole). The Beals and Hoijer contrast between Judaism and Christianity, on the one hand, and all other religions, on the other, with reference to morals has been noted before. The following are more samples:

(1) The Chaga child, in East Africa, must first of all learn the difference between the use of his parents' personal names and the terms of address he must use in speaking to them. This is much the convention of our society, where the child is taught that though his mother addresses his father as "John," he must call him "father" or "daddy" or by some other appelation (Herskovits 1948:320).

(2) Magic is no more the exclusive property of nonliterate peoples than is monotheism the monopoly of certain literate cultures. Goldenweiser has given example after example of the utilization of magic in our culture, masked by the use of other terms. Even though, as he states, it "is no part of our institutionalized religion," yet the sacredness we attribute to holy objects, even the good that is dimly felt accrues through attendance at church and contact with its beneficent powers, is not too far removed from the psychology that places faith in the efficacy of a carved piece of wood, or a rock or a waterfall (Herskovits 1948:360).

(3) A third type of innovation may be called *tentation*. Unlike the previous types, which merely modify or recombine elements of habit already in existence, tentation may give rise to elements that show little or no continuity with the past . . . . Crises are particularly conducive to tentation. In a famine, for instance, people try out all sorts of things that they have never eaten before, and if some of them prove nutritious and tasty they may be added to the normal diet. An epidemic similarly leads to a search for new medicines, and both primitive and civilized peoples have discovered useful remedies in this way. War also leads to improvisation, as do economic crises. The New Deal in the recent history of the United States, for example, reveals numerous instances of tentation. Scientific experimentation, it should be pointed out, is ofter a form of controlled tentation, as when a new series of chemical compounds are systematically put to test. The saying that "necessity is the mother of invention" applies more forcefully to tentation than to invention proper (Murdock 1956:252).

(4) Many economies today lie at an intermediate stage between primitive and developed. There are still in Europe rural communities of farmers who mainly produce for their own needs, but send their surplus products to markets which link them with the world markets of modern capitalism. Through this link they are

---

[8] Just as sociological works have so far largely been confined to American or British or European data, treated as though they are valid for all mankind.

able to acquire tools, machinery, clothing, which they do not produce for themselves. Such dependent economies are found, for example, in rural Ireland, in Poland, and in the Balkans (Forde and Forde 1956:342).

(5) We have thus far been concerned with the matter of whom one may or may not marry. The next question is: "How does a man get a wife?" Very few societies leave it to individuals who are to be married to decide for themselves. The near-anarchy of American practice in this respect is most exceptional, although it represents a discernibly increasing trend in many parts of the world, as the acids of "modernity" corrode the old kinship bonds (Hoebel 1958:344).

(6) Regarding the customary norms for violating the cultural standards: In these examples we see the existence of "pretend rules": standards that are honored in spoken word, but breached in customary behavior. Dry Oklahoma gives us a contemporary American example of what was a national exemplification of a similar situation in the days of federal prohibition of alcoholic beverages (Hoebel 1956:175).

(7) For the Australian natives, as for most of humanity, the local community contains practically all of his society and his culture. Most of the people he knows and cherishes, all the customs, beliefs, and manners which he follows, exist within his local community.

As a matter of fact, it is only in the great new cities of our civilization that the local group has lost some of its importance. A city dweller may not know who lives in the next house or apartment and so can have little feeling for, or participation in, a neighborhood. Perhaps for that very reason there are many efforts, in the form of community centers, local clubs, regional associations, to re-establish the friendly neighborly spirit that was lost in the course of the swift growth of a large city. Many people who now live in cities grew up in congenial, long established neighborhoods, and they miss the loyalties of the local group. Often they transfer their loyalty to the next larger group, the city itself. And they tend to be great boosters for the city and fanatically devoted to such a symbol of the city as, for example, a baseball team like the Brooklyn Dodgers (Mandelbaum 1956:290–291).

(8) Regarding the sexual side of the family life, indeed the limitations may vary to a great extent according to the culture under consideration. In ancient Russia, there was a custom known as *snokatchestvo* whereby a father was entitled to a sexual privilege over his son's young wife; a symmetrical custom has been mentioned in some part of southeastern Asia where the persons implied are the sister's son and his mother's brother's wife. We ourselves do not object to a man marrying his wife's sister, a practice which English law still considered incestuous in the mid-nineteenth century (Levi-Strauss 1956:276).

(9) Around puberty may come *initiation*, which graduates the child from the family circle to more mature status. Such a social and possibly supernatural hurdle may be marked by elaborate instruction and by dramatic symbolism even to the point of physical torture. This period may involve a sharp shift from childhood to adulthood without any recognized intermediate or transitional zone such as is implied in the term "adolescence." Or the transition may be very prolonged—in the Arunta tribe of Australia, to take an extreme instance, some twenty years are required before the rituals to make a man from boy are completed. In modern Western society adolescence is interpreted as a kind of social weaning from the family home setting with an expectation of religious maturity coming early ("confirmation"), political capacity much later ("voting age"), and legal responsibility (no longer being a "minor") variously in between. Among the warrior Masai of east Africa a man is defined as

being at the prime of life between the ages of about eighteen to twenty-six, after which he transfers into the older age group. We may like to be called "youngish" when still in the fifties. It is often said that American society is youth-oriented rather than age-oriented, as are so many other societies (Keesing 1958:248).

(10)   Dowry appears to be a rarer cultural form than bride price. It was apparently very common in Europe, at least among the upper economic strata, but is scarcely represented at all among so-called primitives. The custom has now largely disappeared even in Europe, though the modern custom of providing a bride with household equipment and a stock of new clothing possibly represents a survival of the older cultural pattern (Beals and Hoijer 1965:532).

Many more examples of the same order can easily be found in most anthropological studies, whether they be theoretical or ethnographical. There is nothing wrong with such comparisons if we know the purpose for which they are intended: for example, as useful teaching devices (Albert 1963b). Such comparisons are frequently used by anthropologists who expressly limit themselves to nonliterate societies because these comparisons definitely help the author to elucidate a point more easily and the reader to understand the exotic facts in terms of some familiar context. What is objectionable, from the scientific point of view, is that such comparisons are usually made implicitly or in an offhand manner, or even with unthinking ethnocentrism.

Implicit comparison is far more dangerous than *explicit* comparison. In explicit comparison, the author at least puts himself on record, so that he himself can rationally examine the result of his comparison, and others can judge the factual or logical bases of his comparison as well as the merits or demerits of his comparison. Conscious and systematic comparison is indispensable to anthropology. It also follows that studies of literate civilizations can no more be isolated from incursion into nonliterate societies than vice versa. For practical reasons an anthropologist may have to limit himself to one society at a time, but he should not make a virtue of his limitation, and he has no scientific justification for drawing extensive theories from it.

A less general but even more important reason in favor of the comparative framework is that, unless we can reduce all statements about human behavior to quantitative terms (so that we can speak of 32 degrees of oppression of the Vietnamese government according to Parsons scale, or 105 ounces of affection in the Eskimo marital union according to the Strodtbeck meter, or the like), our qualitative statements about human affairs must be comparative to have any meaning. There simply are no exact measurements which will enable us to see them in absolute terms. For example, how do we measure despotism? How do we measure sibling (or any other) rivalry? How many fights or quarrels or lawsuits must we see for a relationship to be termed rivalrous? And we have to remember that despotism and rivalry are relatively easier entities to gauge than others such as religiosity or prejudice.

In order to be more accurate and to make our statements more meaningful, we must consciously compare the ethnographic data from different societies. We can then say that the political oppression of this society would seem to be greater than that which exists in that one, because a higher incidence of escapism seems to prevail in the former than in the latter, or that the prosperity of one people would seem to have reached a higher level than that of another because the relative unemployment is lower in the former than in the latter. Had students of man really compared the incidence of religious persecution in China and the way Chinese monks and nuns responded to such persecutory efforts with their Western counterparts, they would have perceived the basic difference between Chinese and Western approaches to religion, and we might have had a greatly sharpened scientific understanding of exactly how religion and religious persecution differ with differing patterns of culture, instead of being satisfied with such generalities as "religious persecution is universal," or "religion functions importantly in reinforcing and maintaining cultural values."

Pseudo-comparison and Controlled Comparison

In employing the comparative framework we must, however, keep two precautions in mind. One of these is the differentiation between true comparisons and pseudo-comparisons. A book such as *Six Cultures* (1963), edited by Beatrice B. Whiting, containing accounts of child rearing practices in Kenya, India, Okinawa, Mexico, the Philippines, and the United States, is not a comparative study. It merely puts the six cultures side by side with each other. Erikson's *Childhood and Society* (1950, 1963) is only a comparative study in a limited way. He does begin his book with psychoanalytic histories of an American boy and an adult. From these he proceeds to explore the psychoculture of two American Indian tribes, the Sioux and the Yurok, finally dealing with Americans, Germans, and Russians, but he does not apply his comparative skill to all these societies equally. Instead, he is satisfied with slapdash comparisons. In trying to show the lack of democratic experiences among Germans through an analysis of the childhood of Hitler, Erikson says:

> The other western nations had their democratic revolutions. They, as Max Weber demonstrated, by gradually taking over the privileges of their aristocratic classes, had thereby identified with aristocratic ideals. *There tend to be something of the French chevalier in every Frenchman, of the Anglo-Saxon gentleman in every Englishman and of the rebellious aristocrat in every American.* This something was fused with revolutionary ideals and created the concept of "free man"—a concept which assumes inalienable rights, indispensable self-denial, and unceasing revolutionary watchfulness. For reasons which we shall discuss presently, in connection with the problem of *Lebensraum*, the German identity never quite incorporated such imagery to the extent necessary to influence the unconscious modes of education (1963:333). (Italics mine.)

I have always maintained that Hitler's Naziism was not imposed on the Germans, as some post-World War II apologists would have us believe. And I am therefore not surprised to see signs of resurgence of that ideology in Germany lately, including anti-Semitism. A principal reason is probably that "the concept of 'free man' . . . which assumes inalienable rights, indispensable self-denial, and unceasing revolutionary watchfulness" has not been incorporated into the German educational processes, but Erikson's statement that there is "something of the French chevalier in every Frenchman, of the Anglo-Saxon gentleman in every Englishman and of the rebellious aristocrat in every American" is as absurd as another which claims that every Chinese tends to be a Confucian, or every Sicilian has something of the gangster in him. Such statements distort reality so much that they are harmful even as comparative devices.

Kroeber's *Configuration of Culture Growth* (1944) employed the comparative framework more fully with some resort to quantitative measures. The total number of cultures included is modest by cross-cultural standards. They are generally early Greek, Roman, Italian, Swiss, French, Dutch, British, German, Spanish, Portuguese, Russian, Scandinavian, Polish, and American in the West; Arab-Mohammedan, Egyptian, Mesopotamian, Hebraic, and Byzantine in the Middle East; Indian, Chinese, and Japanese in the Far East, including, as well, the cultures of some countries designated as "marginal nations." His task was to investigate one of the forms that culture takes. "This form is the frequent habit of societies to develop their cultures to their highest level spasmodically: especially in their intellectual and aesthetic aspects, but also in more material and practical respects." Kroeber was specifically interested in "their growth configurations— configurations in time, in space, and in degree of achievement" (1944:5–6).

For this purpose Kroeber examined the waves of development in the fields of philosophy, science, philology, sculpture, painting, drama, literature, and music in these countries. The book gives us many interesting intercultural findings about the fluctuations of peaks and declines in the different fields among various peoples through their known histories. Although eschewing "explanatory" efforts (1944:7), Kroeber nevertheless made a number of interpretative comments such as, "An isolated people will change its culture but is unlikely to produce much that will pass on to others even when the barriers are removed" (1944:676). He cited the cases of Japan and Egypt to support this conclusion.

Kroeber's book is a significant contribution to the comparative approach limited to particular aspects of culture, but it suffers from its avoidance of nonliterate societies. He made no attempt to relate his findings to their possible counterparts in nonliterate societies, probably because of insufficiency or lack of comparable developmental data for nonliterate societies. Nevertheless, we have an interesting example of the onetime dean of American anthropology who, after devoting most of his life to nonliterate societies, took time out to do a sizeable piece of work entirely concentrated on literate civilizations. Kroeber's separatist approach may be interpreted as symptomatic of a conflict between the fact that literate civilizations have so far remained outside of the mainstream of anthropology and a feeling on the part of at least some anthropologists that something needed to be done about them.

Another precaution in using the comparative framework is the absolutely necessary distinction between morphological forms and organizational principles (Boas 1896). We already noted the importance of this distinction in connection with the comparability of religious persecution in Chinese civilization and its counterpart in Western civilization. The two phenomena are not comparable because they were not due to the same causes. The external appearances (morphological forms) were similar. In either case the common fact was that the political authority persecuted people involved in some particular religious belief or organization, but because the underlying causes (organizational principles) were so different, the two patterns of persecutory behavior and the outcomes of the persecution were entirely dissimilar. In addition, the subsequent developments in the two literate civilizations[9] strongly confirmed the importance of this distinction. For while religious persecution disappeared in Chinese history altogether after the T'ang (except for a brief one-year period in 1900), it has continued in Western history even to this day.

The failure to distinguish between morphological forms and organizational principles is a pitfall to which statistically oriented cross-culturalists are especially susceptible, but one from which others who compare less extensively and systematically are not always free. The following schematic treatment of the subject of comparative studies, based upon one by Bohannan (1967:97), is helpful in developing our thoughts on the subject. Bohannan begins with what he describes as a "genealogy" of the various methods that have been used for comparative purposes.

Comparison across Cultures

A. Casual

B. Controlled

(1) Ethnocentric (2) Selected counterilluminative information

(1) Comparison with a standard extrinsic to the particular cultures in hand (2) Controlled variables

(a) Deduced criteria (b) Ethnographically derived criteria

(x) Cross-cultural studies (y) Comparisons in depth

Previously, we have noted many examples of what Bohannan terms here as "casual" and "ethnocentric" (A1) comparison (See pages 79–82). For "casual" and "selected counter-illuminative information" (A2) Bohannan used the example of a Gluckman book on *The Ideas of Barotse Jurisprudence* (1965), where the latter deals with political power and treason. Here, Gluckman, in order to demonstrate his notion that "general ideas of wrong are again best understood in terms of reaction to those wrongs arising in status relations," resorts to sidelights on Zulu, Kalinga, Ifugao, European Middle Ages, Wales, Yorok, England,

---

[9] On this level I am referring to the entire West as being the home of one literate civilization.

Australian Aborigines, Cheyenne, and others. The difficulty is that the comparison is sporadic and diffuse, serving the end not of producing a theory out of the comparative materials but merely of using the positive cases to buttress a position in which Gluckman has entrenched himself.

The concept of "controlled comparison" was first advanced by Eggan (1954). By it Bohannan refers to work which is at once systematic and keyed to the goal of some general theory specially arriving out of all the materials compared. There are two kinds of controlled comparison. "Comparison with a standard extrinsic to the particular cultures in hand" (B1 in the diagram) is the attempt to squeeze the facts of any particular culture into a set of predetermined categories (interrelated or otherwise). Marx's theory of labor versus capital has often been so used in its "applications." The traditional evolutionists also attempted to fit diverse economic facts into a sequence of hunting and gathering, nomadism, and so forth.

The more scientifically legitimate kind of comparison consists of those with "controlled variables" (B2). This can be done by relying on "ethnographically derived criteria" (B2b) or on "deduced criteria" (B1a). The latter come from the scholar's view of the facts or their interrelationship, while the former arise out of the distinctions that are made in the cultures being compared. Bohannan regards the former type of comparison as being less productive than the latter. He likens comparison on the basis of "ethnographically derived criteria" with "the linguist's mode of determining phonemes in any language: if there is a difference in meaning in two sounds, there are two phonemes and hence a legitimate distinction." He believes that this approach enables the investigator "to increase constantly the number of distinctions as more cultures or more intensive materials of known cultures are included."

I do not agree with Bohannan that "deduced criteria" are necessarily "less productive" than "ethnographically derived criteria" because, though language is part of culture, techniques for studying languages and for studying other aspects of culture are not always similar. One obvious difference is that it is infinitely easier to collect linguistic data and to ascertain phonetic and semantic differentiations than to collect cultural data and to determine their interrelationships. The student of cultures must, therefore, have some "view of the facts of their interrelationship" which make up his "deduced criteria" for comparison. So long as these criteria are not too far removed from the ethnographical base, and are revised as they go through successive applications, they will, in fact, be the best available "ethnographically derived criteria" that a culture comparativist can find. (See also Naroll 1962.)

However, the importance of "deduced criteria" goes beyond ethnographic expediency. Overconcentration on "ethnographically derived criteria" may lead to intellectually stultifying results instead of productive ones. The danger is twofold. On the one hand, distinctions only found in a specific culture may be so particular as to be relevant only to its own boundaries. Such distinctions cannot help us in building more generally applicable theories. For example, the Chinese differentiate between two parts in every human soul, a distinction not made by the Japanese. Were this and other Chinese distinctions our only guide, we may be able to achieve a greatly detailed picture of Chinese supernatural beliefs, but we will not advance the cause of comparison.

On the other hand, some distinctions not made in particular cultures are crucial for comparative studies toward the building of more generally applicable theories. For example, the Azande of the southern Anglo-Egyptian Sudan, in common with many other peoples of the world, do not differentiate between the empirical and the magical elements in their view of the causation, or methods of treatment, of illness (Evans-Pritchard 1937:494–498). Once again, were the "ethnographically derived criteria" our only guide, we would not be able to include the Azande culture in our comparison at all. It is only when we employ the "deduced criteria" rooted in cultures other than that of the Azande that we are able to place the Azande case in its proper theoretical perspective.

Therefore, reliance upon "ethnographically derived criteria" may not, as Bohannan believes, enable us "to increase constantly the number of distinctions as more cultures or more intensive materials of known cultures are included." Instead, such an approach may decrease the number of distinctions because some cultures do ignore distinctions made in others. Finally, reliance upon a culture which makes more distinctions than others may merely help us to paint ourselves into a particular corner from which we may find it difficult to emerge.

For these reasons I consider "deduced criteria" and "ethnographically derived criteria" to be equally important. Both can be employed in statistically oriented cross-cultural studies dealing with a few variables (B2bx in diagram) and intensive comparisons in depth of a few cultures dealing with many facets of each (B2by in diagram).

There remains the problem of how to employ the comparative framework, with ethnographically derived criteria, to include both literate societies, with extensive histories and large volumes of written materials, and nonliterate societies, with no written histories and much smaller quantities of such accumulated data, impressions, and interpretations.

8

Postulates as a Solution

T
WO KINDS OF SOLUTION to the problem of comparison will be dealt with in this book. The first is to ascertain the postulates in each society as a basis for comparison and contrast. The postulates are ethnographically derived distinctions made in each culture. In 1954, Hoebel restricted his use of the concept "postulate" to law, but it has a much wider field of application, as he himself showed in his book on the Cheyennes (1960). The second solution is to find a link among different societies (literate and nonliterate) through kinship, the importance of which is deduced. The two solutions deal with two different levels of data. The first tells us something about the focal points in the over-all cultural integration in each society. The second suggests the basic mechanism through which each society manufactures the appropriate psychological responses vis-à-vis its over-all postulates in its new members from generation to generation.

We shall deal with the use of postulates first, resorting to this concept for sketching out a comparative picture among two literate civilizations in the same way Hoebel has done for his nonliterate societies. The two literate civilizations we shall use as our examples are the United States (as an outstanding example of the West) and pre-Communist China (as an outstanding example of east Asia). Before proceeding into this task we must briefly digress by explaining the nature of postulates and how they are derived.

Hoebel begins with the notion, with which we are in accord, that "every society must of necessity choose a limited number of behavior possibilities for incorporation in its culture, and it must peremptorily and arbitrarily reject the admissibility for its own members of those lines of behavior which are incompatible with its selected lines as well as others which are merely different" (Hoebel 1954:12). The criteria governing this choice and rejection usually express themselves as "broadly generalized propositions" (postulates) held by members of every ongoing society "as to the nature of things and as to what is qualitatively desirable and undesirable" (Hoebel 1954:13–14).

The postulates of a culture are not always consistent with each other, but the "measure of consistency" among them and between postulates and "specific selected behavior patterns" will be "the measure of integration of the culture." The responses to specific stimuli on the part of members of any society according to its postulates (or of subgroups within it) not only exhibit patterns of regularity but also carry with them social approval. These are *norms* or *ways* in a society, indicating not only what *is* but also what *ought to be*.[1]

A Note on Method for Deriving Postulates

Hoebel derives his postulates in his nonliterate cultures from a variety of sources, centering in the case method. Primary to his inquiry is the examination of concrete cases that have led to social but especially legal difficulties. After intensive checking for validity of the details, the cases are then "analyzed for what is in them, and compared for what they will yield in generalization (Hoebel 1954: 36).

For example, among the Eskimo not only female infanticide but also killing of the aged who can no longer support themselves are common. There are cases in which a son kills his father at the latter's request and the action incurs *no social disapproval*. Even converted Catholics have done the same. On the basis of such cases Hoebel constructs a postulate and its corollary which read as follows:

POSTULATE. "Life is hard and the margin of safety small."

Corollary. "Unproductive members of society cannot be supported" (Hoebel 1954:69).

This particular Eskimo postulate and its corollary fit in well with the other postulates in the culture. Eskimo culture seems to present no significant internal conflict of postulates, except when some members of the society become Catholics and have to adhere to certain postulates inherent in the Catholic religious culture. For example, one Catholic postulate maintains that taking a life is for God alone. This Catholic postulate is in direct contradiction to the Eskimo postulate and corollary just discussed. Nevertheless, even under such circumstances, Eskimo seem to follow the Eskimo postulate, allowing only a minor Catholic concession, as illustrated by a case in which an ailing husband hangs himself with the help of his wife; both Catholics. "At her husband's request the wife stood by with a crucifix while he (the husband) strung himself up, and just before he expired . . . she released him and held up the cross" (Hoebel 1954:78).

According to Hoebel, "postulates and their derived correlates must always be statements of assumptions as to the nature of things as they exist in the epistemological system of the people whose cultural system is under analysis, and they must "not be mere descriptive summaries of what the people do" (Per-

---

[1] Ruth Benedict had expressed substantially the same ideas in her *Patterns of Culture* (1934:52–61), but Hoebel has refined them into more precise form, and greatly amplified their scientific applicability by introducing the concept of postulates and their corollaries.

sonal communication). Therefore, when observable facts contradict each other and lead to no clear and culturally sanctioned resolutions, the real possibility is that two or more postulates of the culture may be in conflict.

Such a conflict exists, according to Hoebel, between two Cheyenne postulates. One of them is: "Sexual activity should be held to a minimum," under which a wife suspected of being unfaithful could be publicly raped by the husband's military society confreres (at her husband's invitation) and then discarded. However, in all four cases reported, the parties to this punishment did not enjoy public sanction. In fact, "outside intervention blocked the undertaking completely in two cases and by ruse rescued the woman in one other. . . . In all cases the women of the tribe taunted and heckled them for their deed" (Hoebel 1954: 168).

These facts, instead of being evidence for the failure of the Cheyenne to live according to the particular postulate just noted, enables Hoebel to perceive the workings of a conflicting Cheyenne postulate. That latter is: "Women have personal value in their own right" (Hoebel 1954:168).

The data from which I derive the postulates of the two large literate civilizations (the United States and China) include much broader data than case histories could afford, though the latter are useful illustrators and indicators. One reason is that we do not confine ourselves to law. Another reason is that the societies involved are so enormous that I can never hope to collect enough cases for adequate sampling purposes. Fortunately and unavoidably, as pointed out before (see Chapter 6, "Sampling" Problem), we have extensive published materials on both societies by natives and outside observers. The originators of these publications include governments, scientists, literary men, journalists, travelers, and educators.

Consequently, although as anthropologists our central orientation is field investigation, the data from which we derive postulates for these large literate civilizations must come from a variety of sources:

1. Writings on social, religious, and educational philosophies and ethics;
2. Laws and legal trends;
3. Literary works (such as novels) and their most frequent problems and solutions;
4. Advice books and columns;
5. Sociological and anthropological researches;
6. Studies on abnormality, crime, and other forms of breakdown.

In making use of such data it is essential to check one source against another for correspondence or disagreement. Postulates flow from the points of convergence among the various sources.

Besides the sources of information just listed, I must finally add another —namely, personal experience. In my own case, for example, I have had an exceptional opportunity in studying the two literate civilizations under review here. I was born, raised, and educated in China, left it to attend graduate school in England, and returned to it to work and to carry out an intensive field study in one of her major regions. I have never done a field study concentrated in a single community of the West or the United States comparable to the one I did in China; but if we lift our sights and view my activities as a participant observer in the best anthropological tradition, I think my experiences are at least equal to, if not more than, those which may be garnered in several usual field trips. Besides three and a half years in England, I have lived, worked, and raised my children in the United States during the last twenty-three years. My familiarity with Chinese and American histories is not inconsiderable. My command of both languages, written and spoken, is adequate even by rigorous standards. The intensity and extensiveness of my role as a participant-observer of both societies must be considered on the high side compared with those of most anthropological fieldworkers. These living experiences as an active member first of one and then the other of these civilizations not only have provided me with invaluable sources of information but also have served as efficient checks on findings by others and myself as fieldworkers.

The beginning student may react by saying that my type of extensive and intensive personal experience cannot easily be duplicated by others. How can every student be born and educated in one civilization and emigrate and work in another? Actually, my experience is not so unique, seen from one point of view. A majority of our anthropologists are members of literate societies. Each of them has the participant opportunity with his own native society and way of life that I had with the Chinese society and way of life. And all of them have (or will have) carried out intensive fieldwork either in their respective native societies or, more likely, in other areas. Consequently, every anthropologist has (or will have) the opportunity of intensively observing at least two ways of life: the one in which he was raised, educated, and married, and is earning his living, and the one in which he has spent time talking with informants, participating in its ceremonies and rites of passage, and administering tests and questionnaires. Even though many anthropologists will not find direct exploitation of this experience relevant, each one is directly affected by it, and can and should, by attention to the considerations raised in this volume, render use of the experience explicit. This is a very unique resource that anthropology has generally neglected, except at the implicit level, or as represented in unsystematic generalizations that tend to discredit, rather than validate, the significance of the experience.

One common difficulty in studying the patterns of human behavior is, of course, that of differences between ideal and reality. This is especially important in connection with large literate civilizations where the histories are long and facts are complex.

With this in mind it becomes clear that there are ideals which are not postulates (or their corollaries) just as there are postulates (or their corollaries) which are not ideals. "Turn the other cheek" and "Love thy neighbor" are ideals in the American civilization, but not its postulates. Polygyny and the need for officials to take graft are postulates in the Chinese civilization but not its ideals.

In dealing with the postulates which follow, the reader should keep in mind three things. First, our methods for deriving the postulates do not give us *direct proof* of the postulates. Rather, they are deductions from facts (observed behavior or events as well as verbal and written expressions about what were, are, or ought to be). Second, though not directly proven, postulates so derived can serve effectively as points of reference for comparative studies and as framework for more intensified research in each civilization. Third, these postulates for the United States and Chinese civilizations are first approximations. They are, of course, subject to improvements and their adequacy must be measured by how well they can stand up against other formulations which contradict them, but even in their present state, most of them can already serve as guideposts for anticipating or even predicting future developments on a probability basis.

China

POSTULATE I. An individual's most important duty and responsibility are toward his parents, which take precedence over any other interest, including self-interest. The essential expression of this is filial piety. Filial piety is the individual's way of repaying parents for giving him life and raising him.[2]

Corollary 1.[3] An individual must marry and have sons. That is the highest of all filial duties.

Corollary 1'. If his wife gives birth to no son, an individual is justified in marrying a concubine for begetting sons.

Corollary 1''. A sonless man may also fulfill this requirement by adopting a patrilateral cousin's son (father's brother's son's son) or by arranging a matrilineal and matrilocal marriage[4] for one of his daughters. Adoption of unrelated persons is not favored.

Corollary 2. Besides providing heirs, an individual's duty and responsibility toward parents include material support and living together, respect and obedience, proper mourning and burial, care for their souls through worship in the household shrine and clan temple, and glorification of the ancestors by his achievements.

Corollary 3. With reference to their children, parents are always right.

Corollary 3'. Crime against the persons of father or mother is much more heinous than crime against children.

Corollary 3''. By extension, crime against the person of any superior in kinship is more severely punished than crime against inferiors.

Corollary 4. Killing to avenge the murder of a parent is entirely justified. Dying in place of a parent is a high example of filial piety.

---

[2] The reason why we use the present tense for China was explained in Chapter 6, fn. 1.

[3] Corollaries are close logical derivatives directly related to the postulate under which they are subsumed. They must always be next-level abstractions of a more particularistic and detailed nature than the postulate (or, in the case of subcorollaries, of the corollary preceding them) (Hoebel, personal communication).

[4] In anthropological usage matrilocal marriage is one in which a married couple settles in the domicile of the wife's family (this is also called uxorilocal marriage), and the term "matrilineal" usually describes the custom of descent through the mother. The Chinese custom here indicated is somewhat of a variant. It means that not only the husband joins his wife but *he* as well as his children assume the last name of his wife's father.

Corollary 5. While parents are living, an individual must not go far away except with the parents' approval.

Corollary 6. An individual must not knowingly invite danger to his body or life, because to do so means harm to his parents.

Corollary 6'. An individual should not fear danger if it is necessary for the welfare of his parents or approved by them for other purposes (such as support of the government).

Corollary 6''. An individual should do nothing to bring about disgrace to his parents.

Corollary 7. An individual owes everything (including his very life) and all he achieves to his parents and ancestors on the father's side in general. That is why he has to be filial to his parents and never neglect the rites to his ancestors.

Corollary 8. Marriage is the means by which sons continue the family line. A wife must please her husband's parents. A wife who pleases her husband but not his parents should be divorced. Marriage is arranged by the parents. Romantic love is bad. Polygyny for begetting sons is a man's filial duty.

Corollary 8'. Public signs of intimacy between the sexes is indecent under any circumstances.

Corollary 8''. Public demonstration of devotion toward parents (or grief toward their passing or misfortune) is highly meritorious.

Corollary 9. An individual's conduct toward his parents is an invariable guide to his worth in general and for predicting his behavior toward others. (For example, a man who is unfilial to his parents is bound to be treacherous to his friends, colleagues, and employers.)

Corollary 10. A joint family with many generations and married couples under the same roof (same household compound) is a most desirable ideal. Such a joint family is at once an expression of filial piety on the part of the sons and the merit of their ancestors.

Corollary 10'. Harmony among brothers is necessary to achieve and maintain the joint family with many generations and married couples under the same roof. An individual should even subordinate his obligations and feelings toward his wife and children in the interest of fraternal harmony, *especially if his parents are alive.*

Corollary 11. Fathers must provide for sons, including their wives, and see their daughters marry well.

Corollary 11'. An individual's duty and responsibility toward his sisters and daughters will be greatly reduced after they are married into other kinship groups, but those toward his sons will continue indefinitely, as those toward his own parents.

Corollary 12. Ancestral spirits are dependent upon their descendants for offerings and care.

Corollary 13. The individual's achievements are due to merits of departed ancestors.

Corollary 14. Ancestral spirits will continue to look after the welfare of their descendants.

Corollary 14'. Ancestral spirits will not punish their descendants for wrong-doing, but will suffer from them.

Corollary 14''. Ancestral spirits will not take care of the welfare of those who are not their descendants.

Corollary 15. Rulers' ancestral spirits have nothing to do with the people, though rulers have absolute power over the people.

POSTULATE II. All males who are descendants of one common, known ancestor and his spouse and the spouses of these males are members of the same permanent kinship group. They enjoy privileges over and have duties and obligations toward each other in descending degrees of intensity and extent relative to parent-child relationship. This is the Chinese clan. It consists of all of the living, all of the dead males and their spouses, and all of the males yet unborn. All of them, no matter how remote, belong to the same clan temple where rites to all ancestors are periodically performed.

Corollary 1. Within this aggregate of relations, the patrilineage[5] of nine generations (five ascending generations including Ego and five descending generations also including Ego) is the primary social and legal unit, consisting of the dead, the living, and the yet unborn. This unit includes the third patrilateral male cousins (father's father's father's brothers' son's son's sons) in Ego's generation, and second patrilateral male cousins (father's father's father's brothers' son's sons) in grandfather's generation, and so forth. The same gradual reduction of collateral kin rule holds for the descending generations.[6] Figure 8–1 illustrates the Chinese view.

Corollary 2. An individual's duty and responsibility toward the lineage take precedence over those toward the clan, those toward the clan over those toward matrilineal relatives, and those toward matrilineal relatives over those toward nonkin.

Corollary 3. An individual's duty and responsibility toward parents are extended in decreasing order of intensity and relevance to ascending generations of patrilineal ancestors.

Corollary 4. Kinship ties are an individual's most important possession in life, better than wealth. They are preferable to all other ties.

Corollary 4'. An individual who has no living kinship ties is in utmost misery; he is suspect as well.

Corollary 4''. Nonkinsmen are to be treated as kinsmen if business dealings or friendship draw them close. Such persons are drawn closer by marriage of the child of one with the child of the other.

---

[5] A patrilineage is an unilateral kinship group that traces descent from a known common male ancestor who lived not more than five or six generations back. In the Chinese case descent is traced only through males except where a daughter's husband joins her in her own parental household. In that event her husband assumes membership in her kinship group, as we noted before.

[6] In imperial times the ultimate crime, treason, was punishable by execution or banishment of all members of the lineage plus the parents and brothers of the criminal's wife.

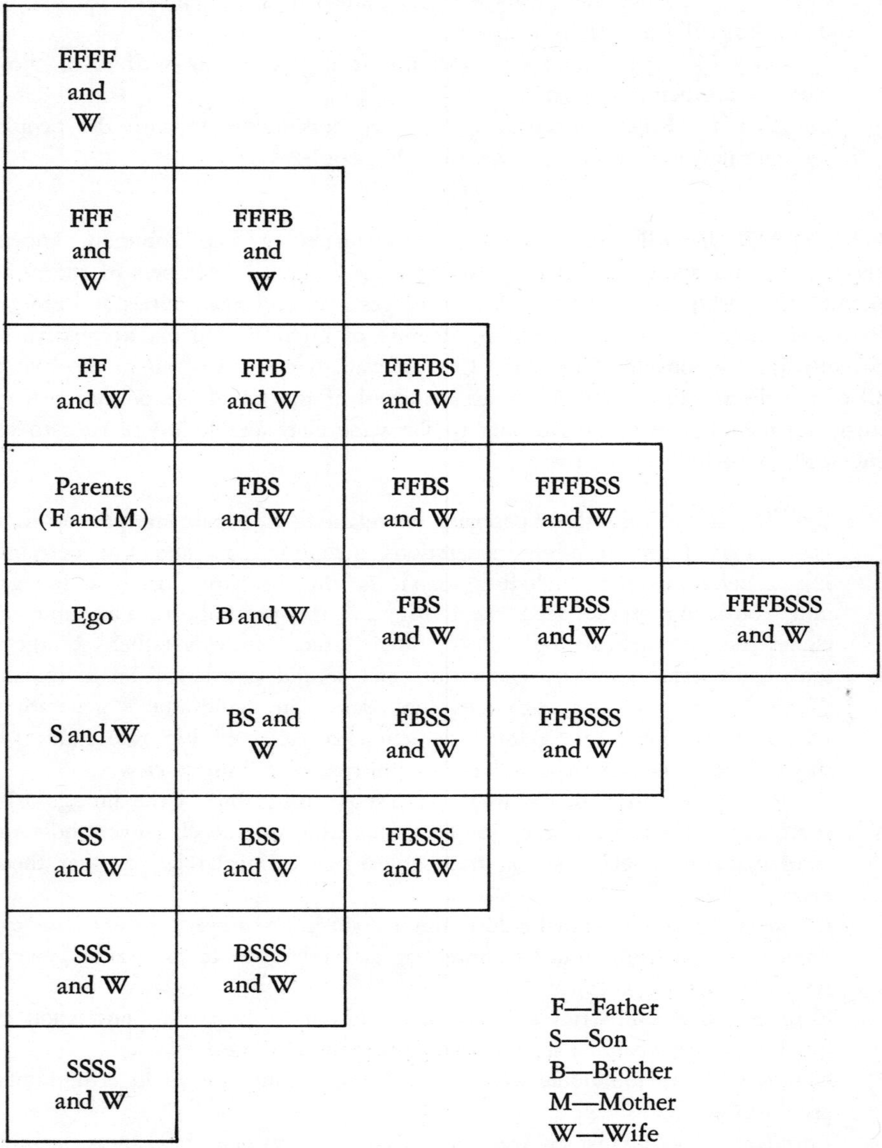

FFFF and W				
FFF and W	FFFB and W			
FF and W	FFB and W	FFFBS and W		
Parents (F and M)	FBS and W	FFBS and W	FFFBSS and W	
Ego	B and W	FBS and W	FFBSS and W	FFFBSSS and W
S and W	BS and W	FBSS and W	FFBSSS and W	
SS and W	BSS and W	FBSSS and W		
SSS and W	BSSS and W			
SSSS and W				

F—Father
S—Son
B—Brother
M—Mother
W—Wife

Figure 8–1

Corollary 5. One should not look for trouble by meddling in other people's affairs except when they are the affairs of one's relatives.

POSTULATE III. All sons are equal, though the eldest has to take the place of the father if the latter dies.

Corollary 1. All sons share the patrimony equally, though the eldest may have a slightly larger share for extra ritual duties (such as tending the graveyard, and so forth).

POSTULATE IV. Women are inferior to men.

Corollary 1. Only men need be given formal education.

Corollary 2. Quarrels among women are unavoidable. Keep them under control.

Corollary 3. A man should not listen to his wife and separate from his brothers.

POSTULATE V. Age means wisdom and deserves respect.

Corollary 1. Younger brothers should obey and respect older ones.

Corollary 2. All younger men should obey and respect all older men within or without the kinship group.

POSTULATE VI. Political rulers are superior to their subjects.

Corollary 1. Rulers make the laws and mete out the punishments.

Corollary 2. Rulers and the people must be separated by wide social and economic gulfs.

Corollary 3. Rulers must rule wisely, justly, and morally.

Corollary 3'. Physical coercion is not as good as moral example and benevolence.

Corollary 4. There are those who naturally can exercise authority over others.

POSTULATE VII. The people are entitled to protection and guidance by the rulers, but the rulers must not interfere with the people in their traditional way of life.

Corollary 1. Rulers must deal sternly and efficiently with large problems such as natural disasters, internal dissension, and external invasion. Otherwise, they will lose their "mandate of heaven" to rule.

Corollary 2. If rulers are unjust and inefficient, the people have the right to revolt.

POSTULATE VIII. Those who work with the brain are superior to those who work with their hands.

Corollary 1. Class distinctions (in wealth, power, intellect, appearance, connections) are necessary and natural. There are bound to be superior and inferior human beings.

Corollary 2. One should help others when they beseech his help, but it is not possible to help all who are miserable, poor, or in trouble.

Corollary 3. Don't fight a man superior by virtue of wealth, power, intellect, or connections until you have carefully estimated your chances of winning.

Corollary 3'. Futile protests are embarrassing and ridiculous.

Corollary 4. What one can accomplish by words one does not do by force.
Corollary 4'. Gentlemen use words but not force.

POSTULATE IX. Gods and ghosts, just as rulers and their officials, exist in a hierarchy and will watch over the people to reward the good and punish the bad.

Corollary 1'. Just as rulers and officials are separated from the people, so are gods and ghosts. Respect the gods and ghosts, but keep them at a distance.
Corollary 1'. Even if you don't believe in gods, you must not be blasphemous.
Corollary 2. An individuals's own ancestral spirits are different from other gods and spirits, though some ancestral spirits, due to meritorious conduct as living beings, may become gods.
Corollary 3. Gods and ghosts may be good or bad. The good gods and ghosts may punish the bad ones. An individual can invoke the good ones to punish the bad.
Corollary 4. Gods are not infallible. They may be fooled.
Corollary 4'. Gods and ghosts may have desires and weaknesses like human beings.

POSTULATE X. The individual should glorify parents, kinsmen, and ancestors by achievements. Parents, kinsmen, and ancestors will all help. It is natural for the individual to need and accept such help.

Corollary 1. Hard work and moral uprightness are necessary for achievement, but the fact that an individual works hard is evidence of the merit of his ancestors (otherwise, they would not have had such good descendants).
Corollary 1'. An individual should help his kinsmen according to the degree of propinquity. To be able to give and to receive such help is evidence of the merit of his ancestors.
Corollary 2. The nature of the ancestral graveyard and ancestral home may be helpful or harmful to the individual's chances for achievement. One should do his best to make sure that these are good. If his achievement is not impressive, the individual can always live up to his place in the kinship group.
Corollary 2'. Contentment will bring everlasting happiness. An individual may not be as good as those whose achievements are above his, but is much better than those whose achievements are below his. It depends upon which way he looks.
Corollary 3. Loyalty to ruler, teacher, employer, and other superiors is good. It does not take precedence over duties and responsibilities to parents and ancestors, but if any good results, it is evidence of ancestral merits.
Corollary 4. The ways of the past were golden. The individual should follow the example of his illustrious ancestors.

POSTULATE XI. Good and evil are relative and will always coexist.

Corollary 1. Avoid evil and keep it under control. It can never be stamped out.

POSTULATE XII. Nonaggression and peaceable ways are better than aggression and strife.

> *Corollary 1.* If a quarrel can be settled amiably, with give and take on both sides, an amiable settlement is infinitely better than a showdown, which always leads to bad blood and sows seeds of future trouble.
> *Corollary 1'.* One who can serve as middleman to pacify quarrels, patch up broken homes, and tie men and women in matrimony is highly meritorious.
> *Corollary 1".* A gentleman is sociable but not partisan. A small man (common man) is partisan but not sociable.

POSTULATE XIII. Reciprocity *(pao)* is the invariable law which operates among all gods, men, and things.

> *Corollary 1.* The meritorious will be rewarded with good *pao*. Those who are undutiful, bad, or evil will be punished accordingly with bad *pao*.
> *Corollary 1'.* Reward or punishment may come slowly, in roundabout ways, in one's future reincarnations or to one's descendants.
> *Corollary 2.* Filial piety is the sons' (and/or daughters') way of repaying their debt to their parents, who gave them life and raised them. Meritorious parents will have filial sons.
> *Corollary 2'.* A similar kind of link between merit and reward or demerit and punishment pertains, to varying extent, to all human relationships.
> *Corollary 3.* The cause-effect relationship between action and *pao* may be changed by additional merit or demerit. Good *pao* may turn into bad *pao* if the person who is entitled to it misbehaves. Bad *pao* may likely be turned into good *pao* for the same reason in reverse.

POSTULATE XIV. China is the oldest country in the world and the Chinese way of life is superior, but there are many Chinese who are ignorant and inferior (human beings are not equal), just as there are many non-Chinese peoples who do not share the Chinese ways.

> *Corollary 1.* If non-Chinese peoples want to learn the Chinese ways they are welcome. It will not be easy, but many have done so in the past.
> *Corollary 2.* There are peoples who will never learn the Chinese ways. It is not our business to bother about them.

The reader who is interested in ample documentation for these postulates and corollaries of the Chinese civilization can satisfy his curiosity in three of my books: *Under the Ancestors' Shadow* (1948, 1967), *Americans and Chinese: Two Ways of Life* (1955),[7] and *Clan, Caste and Club* (1963). The data on

---

[7] A revised version of this book will be published in 1968 under the title *Americans and Chinese: Passage to Understanding*; New York: Natural History Press. For a brief discussion of what the Chinese Communist Revolution since 1949 means to the Chinese civilization and its postulates, see discussion, later in this chapter.

China were collected from a variety of sources: field and other scholarly reports, literature and folklore, historical documents [including District Gazeteers (Hsien Chih)], and popular media such as newspapers and mass circulating magazines. For example, all of these sources massively support our postulate I and its corollaries. To begin with, the Chinese not only have a *Filial Piety Classic* (*Hsiao Ching*) but also at least two series of *Twenty-Four Examples of Filial Piety*. The latter are also dramatized on the stage and were serialized as late as the 1930s in comic-like strips. Their themes vary from a man who melted the ice in a frozen river with his bare body so that fish jumped in response to his step-mother's wish for some fish, to a girl who sold herself into slavery in order to give her father a proper funeral.

Some of these "examples" (and certainly many of the details) were, of course, no more based on facts than Roy Rogers' always immaculate performance in American Western movies, but the kind of themes the Chinese have responded to for so many centuries are unmistakably consonant with their traditional laws and customs, their institutions and kind of heroes' problems as they see them, and solutions as their newspaper advice column writers offer. For instance, the following is a letter addressed to a North China newspaper counselor, and the latter's reply. This was in 1946, two years before the rise of Communism.

Dear Mr.————:

The wheel of time marches on. Circumstances change continuously. I, too, am one of those who is looking for a way out. Sir, I am a seventeen-year-old school girl. Two years ago I made a friend of the opposite sex. In age and education he is equal to me. We saw each other frequently during the last two years. While our impressions of each other deepened, we remained on the level of platonic friendship. We never talked about the word love when we saw each other, therefore I trust him deeply and respect him very much. This last summer he proposed to me. I said yes. When I returned home I told my parents about it. Now my father is a conservative man; he absolutely refused. I have been living in a sea of bitterness for the last months.

Recently this man wrote me a letter in which he said, "You ought to break with this conservative family. For our future happiness you ought to be courageous and not weaken." Then this man walked back and forth in front of our house. When he saw me, he asked me to write an essay on "The Story of My Struggle." But who can understand? Physically my father is very weak, he is also bothered by high blood pressure. My reverend one cannot stand a big shock. I told this man about it, but he is not sympathetic toward this view. He comes around daily and gives me no peace.

I cannot think of any way out. I know of one way out that will solve all the problems, which is suicide. Although I know that suicide is the road of the weak, I think I am a weak one. Sir, what do you think of this as a way out? If I do so, will that not be bad for the name of the family? If I do so, what will he do? Kindly point out to me a road bright and clear. If you can do that, my gratitude to you will last forever.

(Signed) ————

Dear ————:

Man is not a plant. He has emotions. Emotion has no limit. Young men and women too youthful in their outlook are usually troubled by emotions. However, when you talk about marriage as soon as your emotions are aroused, you are likely to run into many dangers.

If you really considered the matter rationally, you should realize that although your two hearts agree with one another and your emotions are deep, you do not have to marry right away so as to complicate matters. Marriage ought to be determined, of course, by the two partners concerned, but when you consider your unsatisfactory family environment and the high blood pressure of your father, you ought to take it easy in order to avoid a possible tragedy. Your thought that suicide will end all comes from over-narrowmindedness, for which you will be adversely criticized by society.

My practical advice now is that, if you really love each other, and if you have both made up your mind on your common objective, you will do best by being engaged to each other secretly just between yourselves. After a period of time you can then ask someone to talk the matter over with your parents. You will find that then it will only be a matter of form, that the storm will die and the tides will ebb and all problems will be solved. I hope you will follow this advice and do not think of suicide.

The basic views of the girl and the counselor agree with each other. The crux of the matter is not that her parents were unfavorable to the marriage, a situation not uncommon in the United States and the world over, but from the American point of view the Chinese girl lacked the determination of a woman in love. Even when she contemplated suicide, she was still concerned with the family name. And the counselor, though already Westernized to the extent of admitting the desirability of individual choice in marriage, advised her to wait patiently and indefinitely.

In a survey of three major and one minor newspapers in the Tientsin and Peking (then Peiping) area between 1945 and 1948 I found scores of other replies to letters which suggested and insisted in one way or another that affections between the sexes should take second place not only to parental wishes (some even dwelled on the importance of the opinion of sisters and in-laws) but also to the demands of work and education.

Illustrative of the latter attitude are the public responses to a letter (in the same group of papers surveyed) by a young lady which begins with the caption: "Fellow Sisters, Beware of Men." She was nineteen years old and in her last year of high school.[8] Her tale of woe was this: She was introduced at a ball to a handsome, college-educated, young army officer. Thereafter, the two of them made the rounds of the city. However, when sometime later she hinted at marriage, he made no response at all. Shortly afterward he stopped seeing her altogether. As a result, she felt badly cheated ("Everybody laughed at me"), and she advised her female readers to beware of such irresponsible wolves.

An avalanche of letters came to the newspaper as a result. These came from students and the general public. The basic uniformity of their orientation was surprising. Some sympathized with her. Some accused her of vanity and of forgetting that boyfriends are not for high school girls. Some said she had no business dancing when "only nineteen." Some defended army officers in general, even though they conceded that this particular one was inconsiderate. But none of

---

[8] Up to the Communist triumph there was no compulsory education in China. A nineteen-year-old in high school was not at all unusual.

them questioned her right to expect marriage, and all of them reiterated: Now that you have your medicine, be rational, give up pleasures, and concentrate on your studies. Her goal should be to finish school with flying colors, enter college, and work toward a great career. Some literally asked her to repent.

To make the process of deduction more explicit let us examine the facts more closely. The first case may be dissected into the following elements:

A. Seventeen-year-old girl met a boy of suitable age and comparable education.

B. The two dated for two years and she was now 19.

C. He proposed marriage and she accepted.

D. Her father refused to accept the match.

E. The young man became bitter because she would not go against her father's wishes.

F. She spoke of suicide.

G. She worried about what her suicide would do to the good name of her family.

H. Newspaper columnist advised her to keep engagement secret and to wait because of her father's weak heart.

I. He also advised her that if she did not wait she would be criticized by society.

J. Finally, he advised her to get some peacemaker to smooth her way with her parents in the hope that they would agree.

Items A, B, C, D, and F can occur in any society. Items E and, especially, G are expressions of postulates I and its corollaries 3, 5, 6″, and 8 in the Chinese civilization. Items H and I confirm the postulate and the corollaries named. Item J is an expression of postulate XII, especially its corollaries 1 and 1′.

The elements of the second Chinese case give support to and dovetail with the postulates and corollaries derived from those of the first one. Here the facts may be itemized as follows:

K. Nineteen-year-old high school girl met a handsome, college-educated, young army officer.

L. The two dated.

M. She fell in love with him and hinted at marriage.

N. He did not reciprocate.

O. He stopped seeing her.

P. She was angry and turned sour against all men.

Q. Other readers advised her that as a high school girl she had no business making friends with men, or dancing with them.

R. Other readers told her to concentrate on study and forget about boys, work toward a great career.

S. Still others told her to repent.

Once again items K, L, M, N, O, and even P can occur in any society. But items Q, R, and S contain advice that she should not only wait till much older, but perhaps never do any of these (postulate I, corollaries 8 and 8'). Implicit in the advice is the idea that her marriage would eventually be taken care of by her father (postulate I, corollary 11).

The small amount of data given here can also serve as an instrument for elucidating certain postulates and corollaries in US civilization. Western readers will get the best results by putting themselves in the position of the Chinese letter writers or respondents, writing out the kind of letters or responses that they would have considered rational, logical, or desirable, and then comparing the results with what I have taken from the Chinese scene.

For Westerners items A, B, C, and D are common enough. Even item E is not improbable, but for them item G tends to be irrelevant (see US postulate I, corollary 5). Item H may or may not hold for the Westerner. It will be a matter of individual adjustment. One can find some American daughters who ruined their chances of marriage because of their fathers (or sons because of their mothers). However, item I will not hold true for Westerners, and item J will look ridiculous to them. A clergyman or a psychiatrist may be asked to intervene on some personal matters, but an ordinary peacemaker's efforts in the situation presented here would only be seen as interference and therefore undesirable.

To Westerners items K, L, M, N, and O in the second Chinese case are familiar enough, but they will find items Q, R, and S absolutely unacceptable. Furthermore, Western readers are unlikely to write as did their Chinese counterparts, not only because they would disagree with the views expressed but also because they would regard expressing their opinions on such matters as intrusion of the original writer's privacy. Postulate I, corollaries 4, 4', 5, and 6 and postulate II of the US culture are contrary to items Q, R, and S.

The same process of deduction may be illustrated by an American example which we shall scrutinize with an American eye and then with its Chinese counterpart. What follows is an episode from an American movie that I saw a few years back. I have also included the audience reaction to it.

A young couple had a quarrel. The wife, in a huff, ran out of the apartment carrying a packed suitcase. The husband's mother, who lived on the next floor, then appeared on the scene. The elderly woman consoled her son by saying, "You are not alone, son; I am here." The audience roared with laughter. The sequence of events and the particular remark left no doubt in the minds of the audience that the elder woman was the cause of the young couple's quarrel. The mother was committing the worst of follies because she did not have sense enough to stay away, especially after the trouble had flared into the open.

The data are:

A. A young couple had a quarrel.

B. The wife ran out of the house with her suitcase.

C. Husband's mother came to the scene to console her son.

D. Older woman said, "You are not alone, son; I am here."

E. Audience roared with laughter at older woman's remark.

F. Film maker showed mother committing the worst of follies and the audience agreed with the film maker.

Items A and B are not unusual in both Chinese and US cultures. Item C is less common and certainly less acceptable in the US culture than in Chinese culture. This signified the strength of the US postulate I, corollary 1″ and corollary 5′. The US postulate and corollaries express themselves much more forcefully in items D, E, and F, which will have contrary significance for a Chinese audience. In the Chinese view, the younger woman, and not the older one, would have been the culprit. For whether or not a man has reached majority, his tie with his parents customarily has priority over that of the marital bond (Chinese postulate I, corollaries 1, 1″, 5, 8, 8′, 8″, and 10).

Three critical questions may be directed at the procedure for deriving postulates and their corollaries. First, how does a student begin to fix his eyes on some fact or cluster of facts in a culture and decide that it can serve as the basis of one or more postulates and corollaries?

My answer is a twofold one: On the one hand, the student must have an intensive familiarity with the culture in question by traditional anthropological fieldwork. This familiarity may be deepened, as we noted before, by systematic comparison between the anthropologist's field culture and his home culture. A student not equipped with this familiarity but merely trained in modern sociological or psychological techniques will not be able to do this. On the other hand, even though intensively acquainted with the culture, the anthropologist still has to go through a process of trial and error very much in the manner that an arithmetician doing division would go about finding suitable, correct quotients. For example, when the arithmetician tries to divide 4515 by 129, he may have to begin with 2 or 4 before settling down to 3. Unless the person is very ignorant of numbers, he is not likely to start out with 6 or 1. This is the kind of beginning that all anthropologists familiar with his culture must make. He takes that step by a combination of knowledge and insight.

Once having made the beginning, the anthropologist is ready to explore further. That first finding then becomes his initial postulate (or hypothesis) with which to order other relevant data. As he proceeds to do so, he may have to modify the first postulate, add to it, subtract from it, or eliminate it altogether. Here we must deal with a second question: How do we know that the data given are not misinterpreted or overweighted because of the student's preconceived notions on what should have been the postulates and corollaries in the first place?

My answer to this question is that other sources of information (see discussion earlier in this chapter) concerning the culture in question must support the postulates and corollaries derived. In our present exercise data for our Chinese postulates and their corollaries are found not only in newspaper advice columns and letters but also in novels, poetry, honored classics, school texts, district gazeteers, genealogical books, religious precepts, and field research results. The US postulates and their corollaries, which we shall outline later, were derived from an equally great variety of data.

Furthermore, once having isolated a number of postulates and their corollaries in any culture, the student will continue to discover new facts which bear on them. For example, when I was preparing *Americans and Chinese: Two Ways of Life* (1953), I did not see the extent to which Chinese and Westerners differed in their approach to mythology. I have now done more work in this area and have found a great deal of additional evidence relevant to the contrast between US self-reliance and independence from parents (US postulate I and corollaries) and Chinese stress on mutual dependence and subordination to parents (Chinese postulate I and corollaries). I shall indicate here the differential treatments of the primeval Deluge by Western and Chinese myth makers, which strongly support this contrast.

The Western reader is generally familiar with the sequence of events after Noah was informed of the impending disaster by God. His solution was to pack up his wife, his three sons, and their wives, and pairs of all animals in a ship to escape the disaster. When the flood subsided, they landed on Ararat. After thanking the Lord by appropriate rituals Noah and his wife apparently lived for a while with his sons and their wives together. Then Noah drank the wine he made and, while under the influence of liquor, he masturbated in his tent. Ham, seeing his father exposed, told his two brothers about it; the sons were all disgusted with Noah. There ensued some kind of quarrel, and Noah then blessed Shem and Japheth, cursed Ham, and condemned Ham's son Canaan to be their slave. The sons and their wives then dispersed to different parts of the earth.

The Chinese account is briefly as follows: Emperors Yao and Shun (said, respectively, to have reigned 2358–2257 B.C. and 2258–2206 B.C.) were great and moral rulers. In Yao's old age a terrible flood devastated the country. Yao appointed an official to control the flood, but the official was unsuccessful. Yao decided to appoint the able and popular man Shun as his successor to the throne. Emperor Shun exiled the official who failed to control the flood and appointed the exile's son Yu in his place. Yu worked for many years, going all over the country, and succeeded in finally eradicating the flood. During his many years of duty he passed by his own house three different times (during the first year of his absence his wife gave birth to a son), but he was so mindful of his duty that he did not enter it even once. After his success, Yu was appointed the next emperor by a grateful Shun. Thus, Yu not only vindicated his father but also brought great honor to his father.

Throughout the two mythological sequences, the Western one is centered upon the individual and his spouse, moving away from the homeland and from traditional authority, dispersing into different parts of the world, while the Chinese one emphasizes the group and traditional authority, staying in the same area, and continuation of the father-son tie. The Chinese approach to the Deluge in myth was later to be sharpened, throughout historical times, by Confucius and his followers, in their glorification of filial piety. It is equally interesting that the Western approach to the Deluge in myth was later translated and specified by Jesus when he propounded the following and other similar ideas:

> And the brother shall deliver up the brother to death, and the father the child: and the children shall rise up against *their* parents, and cause them to be put to death (Matthew 10:21).

> Think not that I am come to send peace on earth: I came not to send peace, but a sword (Matthew 10:34).

For I am come to set a man at variance against his father, and the daughter against her mother, and the daughter-in-law against her mother-in-law (Matthew 10:35).

The third and final critical question that may be directed toward our procedure is, in attempting to derive and substantiate the postulates and their corollaries, are we not often guilty of selecting and arranging our data to suit our purposes? To this question my answer is, first of all, "Yes." No scientific study can use all data without discrimination. Even a descriptive monograph of a single village must perforce be restricted in its coverage. A complete coverage of all facts about all Hindu India or any other large literate society is an impossibility. The only practical criteria for judging the soundness of the selection are these: (1) Do the selected data make sense in terms of the postulates and corollaries they are supposed to support? (2) Are there significant or obvious facts of comparable order which contradict them but which have been left out? The significance of the first criterion is obvious. Upon the second criterion rests the distinction between demonstrating a point and illustrating it. In demonstrating a point the adequacy of the work is measured not only by how well it is supported by the data assembled but also by how well it can stand up against other data which contradict it. The critics of any such work must do more than merely voice dissatisfaction on the general ground that the facts are selected. They must be able to advance other facts, show how their new facts are contradictory to the postulate or corollary demonstrated, or how their new facts can lead to an alternative postulate or corollary which is central to the civilization in question.

We are now ready to state some of the postulates and corollaries of the US civilization. Once again, I have to note that extensive documentation for these constructs lies elsewhere. The reader should consult not only two of my three books listed before (1955, 1963, 1968) but also the writings of de Tocqueville (1862, 1945), Riesman (1950), Commager (1950), Lipset (1963), and Henry (1963). These students (and a number of others) on American national character and civilization are by no means in complete agreement with each other, but the reader will have little difficulty in steering an intelligible course for himself if he follows our postulates and their logical deductions.

The United States

POSTULATE I. An individual's most important concern is his self-interest: self-expression, self-development, self-gratification, and independence. This takes precedence over all group interests.

> Corollary 1. After self-interest the individual's responsibility toward his wife and minor children (in that order) takes precedence over all else.
> Corollary 1'. Parents must cultivate the friendship of their children and keep communication lines with them open.
> Corollary 1''. Parents should assist but not interfere with their children, especially when the youngsters have married or reached majority.

Corollary 2. The individual has little responsibility toward his parents and no responsibility toward other kinsmen.

Corollary 3. Upon reaching majority an individual is free to do anything, form or join any group, and go anywhere that is not illegal.

Corollary 4. An individual should seek the good life and pursue happiness.

Corollary 4'. The good life and happiness consist primarily of the maximization of bodily comforts, food, and sexual enjoyment. Pursuit of knowledge for its own sake and worship of God through eternal abstention and asceticism are not favored. Health and sexual attractiveness must be defended at all costs.

Corollary 4". Altruism is examined for ulterior motives.

Corollary 5. Selection of a mate is the concern of the individual partner only, for marriage is for individual happiness.

Corollary 5'. Sex must be based on love.

Corollary 5". Marital affairs are matters for the marital partners alone. Parents should stay out.

Corollary 6. An individual must decide on his own career or occupation and advance on his own.

Corollary 6'. An individual is responsible for his own actions unless he is a minor or insane.

Corollary 7. Individual initiative, excellence, and creativity are highly desirable.

Corollary 7'. Individual ambition and competition are highly desirable virtues.

Corollary 7". To be content is to stagnate, to be uncreative, and to be unworthy.

POSTULATE II. The privacy of the individual is the individual's inalienable right. Intrusion into it by others is permitted only by his invitation.

Corollary 1. An individual's body is inviolate.

Corollary 2. An individual's property is inviolate.

Corollary 2'. Violation of property is to be punished severely.

Corollary 3. An individual's conscience is to be respected.

Corollary 3'. Conscientious objection to serving the country is possible.

Corollary 4. Sharing one's private life is a costly matter. Since all close relations contain limitations, it is often better to share one's personal life with strangers or paid servants (for example, analysts, psychiatrists, or counselors).

POSTULATE III. Because the government exists for the benefit of the individual and not vice versa, all forms of authority, including government, are suspect. But the government and its symbols should be respected. Patriotism is good.

Corollary 1. Sacrifice for the government is only justified during a national emergency.

Corollary 1'. An individual may be partially excused from this sacrifice if his conscience forbids it.

Corollary 2. The government should protect the individual, thereby justifying its existence.

Corollary 3. The government should not encroach upon the freedom and privacy of the individual.

Corollary 4. The government should be run by representatives chosen by and from among the people.

Corollary 4'. The people in government are the same as ordinary people.

Corollary 5. People with great power are likely to have better ways of furthering their own self-interests. They are likely to act contrary to the general good.

Corollary 6. The people must watch the government and check it when it misbehaves or fails to deliver the goods.

Corollary 7. Broad charisma (popular appeal) is important for leaders in government. This means they must be responsive to the people's needs. Even actors, television personalities, and even professional athletes may become political "leaders."

POSTULATE IV. An individual's success in life depends upon his acceptance among his peers.

Corollary 1. An individual must combine with peers to further his self-interest.

Corollary 2. An individual must maintain his flexibility for vertical or horizontal mobility by not being involved too much with specific peers at any time.

Corollary 3. Being a member of exclusive clubs is the most important sign of the individual's success.

Corollary 3'. Nothing succeeds like success among one's peers.

POSTULATE V. An individual should believe or acknowledge God and should belong to an organized church or other religious institution. Religion is good. Any religion is better than no religion.

Corollary 1. Individuals who do not belong to churches are socially abnormal.

Corollary 1'. Individuals who deny the existence of God or who think churches are bad are suspect.

Corollary 2. There is only one God.

POSTULATE VI. Men and women are equal.

Corollary 1. There are developmental differences between the sexes.

Corollary 2. There are differing needs between the sexes.

Corollary 3. Men and women should receive the same formal education, occupational considerations, etc.

POSTULATE VII. All human beings are equal.

> *Corollary 1.* Differences of race, class, national origin, religion, education, and natural attributes make people unequal, but with each generation these inequalities are reduced. Social inequality is temporary.
>
> *Corollary 2.* Education will serve to make people more equal.
>
> *Corollary 3.* Inequalities in occupational prestige and salaries are consistent with the value placed on individual initiative, and legitimate as long as individual opportunities for achievement are equal.

POSTULATE VIII. Progress is good and inevitable. An individual must improve himself (minimize his efforts and maximize his returns); the government must be more efficient to tackle new problems; institutions such as churches must modernize to make themselves more attractive.

> *Corollary 1.* Education and its elaboration are absolutely good. Education is one of the two chief means for all kinds of progress .
>
> *Corollary 2.* Wealth and its increase are absolutely good. Wealth is the other chief means for all kinds of progress.
>
> *Corollary 2'.* Most or all problems can be solved by judicious monetary appropriations.
>
> *Corollary 2''.* A great deal of any appropriation should go to research (physical, medical, industrial, psychological, and even sociological) which will bring about progress.
>
> *Corollary 3.* Good and evil each are absolute. They cannot coexist. However, the world is temporarily divided between good and evil. Progress means the systematic extermination of evil by the good.
>
> *Corollary 4.* Youth is good. The future is before the young. Old age is bad. Old people have no role in the scheme of things.
>
> *Corollary 4'.* Opinions and wishes of children are to be taken more seriously than those of the elderly.
>
> *Corollary 4''.* Crimes against children are more heinous than those against adults.
>
> *Corollary 5.* The fight against evil requires the active participation of everyone.

POSTULATE IX. Being American is synonymous with being progressive, and America is the utmost symbol of progress.

> *Corollary 1.* The United States has a mission to spread Americanism to all peoples of the world.
>
> *Corollary 2.* Obstructions to the spread of Americanism are intolerable and must be destroyed (by war, if necessary) until the good prevails.
>
> *Corollary 3.* Americans are willing to go a long way to help those who acknowledge the superiority of Americans and Americanism, so that they will become Americanized.

Corollary 3'. Americans have the power and know-how to build the world anew, where the weak will be protected.

As pointed out previously, substantive discussion of the postulates for both civilizations may be found in my book *Americans and Chinese: Two Ways of Life* (1955). We also noted before that the traditional Chinese way of life has not been abruptly and totally changed by the Communist revolution of 1949, as popularly imagined. The Communist revolution has attempted to make and has made some great dents in the traditional way of life, but it is a successor to previous movements in the same direction such as the Nationalist Revolution of 1928 and the Republican Revolution of 1912. Each of these shook up China to a degree and each prepared the way for the succeeding one. The year 1949 merely marked the beginning of a new phase of forced changes in the Chinese way of life under external pressure.

The changes attempted or effected were and are basically not of Chinese origin, and many of them are commensurate with the postulates of American civilization rather than those of the Chinese. At the core of this thrust for change is the effort to remove the all-pervasive influence of the kinship group centering in one's duties and responsibilities toward one's parents (Chinese postulates I and VIII) and the unequalness of male and female (Chinese postulate III). In addition, attempts are also made to reduce or eliminate the traditional superiority of those who work with the brain vis-à-vis those who work with the hand (Chinese postulate VI) and the age-old beliefs in gods and ghosts (Chinese postulate VII). Nationalism and industrialization are the two outstanding aims of the revolutionary governments of China. These aims are impossible of fulfillment unless the Chinese are pried loose from their kinship ties so that they can freely combine with other individuals on economic, technical, and, especially, political and ideological bases.

In steering the Chinese toward the latter course the Chinese leaders have found some traditional postulates instrumental. For example, Chinese postulate V, "Political rulers are different from their subjects," and its corollaries have made their exercise of authority in the short run much easier than might otherwise have been the case. Chinese postulate IV, "Age means wisdom and deserves respect," has made it possible for old Chinese leaders to continue their power and influence beyond what most of their Western counterparts can enjoy. Chinese postulate X, "China is the oldest country in the world and the Chinese way of life is superior," provides some foundation and substance for the Chinese Communist claim to and drive for supremacy in the Communist world.

However, the same Chinese postulate X is also a stumbling block to easy acceptance of many changes of Western origin, as are also the other postulates which the revolutionary leaders seek to reduce or eliminate. In one way or another the traditional Chinese postulates will tend to assert themselves or to reappear in disguise. Though the latest and the strongest revolution so far, the Communist revolution is far from complete, or it would not have the need for indoctrinations, public confessions, forced population movements, and, more recently, the Red Guards.

The American reader may appreciate the Chinese situation a little better if he will reflect on the history of race relations in the United States. The Civil War of 1861–1865 technically abolished slavery in all of the Union, but not only did it not abolish the hierarchical gulf between Negroes and whites in the South, it only made the *de facto* racial castelike pattern in the North somewhat less obvious. One hundred years after that momentous Civil War and official abolition of slavery we are still prevented by all sorts of legal, social, educational, and economic barriers from realizing a situation anywhere near Negro-white equality. Racially motivated murders, riots, demonstrations, and counterdemonstrations leading to varying degrees of violence have filled the news throughout the 1960s and more promise to come.

The general public and newspaper reporters in America often tend to perceive the world situation in terms of absolutes, reacting to other, especially distant lands, by viewing them as either completely unchanging or totally changed; however, the student who knows something about the actual processes of social and cultural transformation realizes that speed and clean-cut breaks are not characteristic of such processes. The American Civil War was preceded by many expressions against slavery and is still followed by violence a century after complete military victory of the Abolitionists. The Chinese Communist Revolution of 1949 was similarly preceded by various eruptions, and we have so far seen only a fraction of the eruptions which will certainly come after it.

The only difference between the two situations is this: The American Civil War was, and the struggles which followed it that we are witnessing today are, an intrinsic expression of the American postulate for progress (US postulate VIII) indigenous to the American civilization, so that it and the following eruptions are in line with most of the other postulates of the American civilization, but the Chinese Communist Revolution, like its predecessors the Nationalist and Republican revolutions, received its impetus from Western pressure and its inspiration from Western sources, so that it, its predecessor, and successor eruptions are in conflict with most of the other postulates of the Chinese civilization, and, therefore, in many ways harder to effect because they necessitate greater changes in fundamentals.[9]

We now turn to the second solution to the problem of how to employ the comparative approach to best advantage in the study of literate civilizations—that of the study of kinship.

---

[9] For an analysis of the extent of change necessary, and the deep difficulties involved in the Chinese revolution, see Hsu (1966c, 1968c).

9

Study of Kinship as a Solution

KINSHIP IS AT THE CORE of all social organization. This universality of kinship links all societies, large and small, literate or nonliterate. Yet kinship is not a superficial matter or a mere decoration. It plays a central role in the upbringing of the human individual in every society. The individual encounters kinship at the beginning of his life and it continues to be important during a considerable period after he is born. This is the period when the individual is most helpless and yet when his ability and speed of learning are much higher than in later periods. Kinship is the base from which, or by means of which, the individual launches his relations with nonkin and either rejects it in favor of other groups or builds other groups on top of it. It provides him especially with the necessary psychosocial tools with which he will deal with the larger worlds of man, gods, and things in consonance with the major postulates of his society and culture accumulated from the past.

If we think of a germ cell (a fertilized egg) as providing the basic biological materials out of which the organism develops in conjunction with a variety of congenital and postnatal forces originating from the environment, we can conveniently regard the elementary kinship unit (whether in terms of some form of the nuclear family or the matrilocal household of the mother, mother's brother, and unmarried children) as the core structure which is the "cultural organization of emotional and intellectual processes" (Hunt 1965:7) and supplier of the basic psychic and social materials out of which the individual personality [or Kardiner-Linton's "basic personality" and Kaplan's "social personality" (Kaplan 1954, 1961)] develops in conjunction with a variety of economic, political, and cultural factors particular to his society.[1]

The study of kinship dates back almost to the beginning of the history of anthropology. Kinship studies have produced, or are interrelated with, many high points in methodology and theory. Murdock's landmark book *Social*

---

[1] These and other environmental factors, of course, affect at all times the basic kinship unit as well as the personality of the individual as the latter grows.

Structure (1949) is one of the best examples. It has enabled us to see a variety of links (in the form of correlations) between lines of descent and those of inheritance, forms of marriage and rules of incest, and so forth. However, after being a focus of anthropological productivity the study of kinship has not been as helpful to our understanding of human behavior as its central importance in human development necessarily leads us to expect. We have yet to see the social and cultural significance of the fact that the Eskimo, the Yankees of New England, the peasant Ruthenians of eastern Europe, the agricultural Taos Pueblo, and the Andamanese Pygmies, among others, share one kind of kinship structure, while the Fijians, the Tallensi, the Manchus, and the Chinese, and others, share another (Murdock 1949: 226–228, 236–238). The striking thing is that the diverse peoples so grouped together have few other behavioral and cultural characteristics (from religion to politics) in common, despite their similarity in kinship structure. In this regard the mathematical models of kinship such as those of White (1963) have not helped us.

The reason why kinship has not yielded more results to elucidate our understanding of social and cultural patterns is, in my view, due to the concentration on kinship structure to the neglect of kinship content. To explicate the differences between structure and content, however, it is necessary for us to introduce four terms: "dyad," "attribute," "dominant dyad," and "dominant attribute." They may be defined as follows:

A *dyad* is a minimum unit into which two persons are linked. Thus, a father-son relationship, a relationship between two friends, and an employer-employee relationship are all examples of dyads. In the nuclear family we find a number of such dyads as: husband-wife, father-son, mother-son, brother-brother. *Attribute* refers to the characteristic quality of inteaction and attitude intrinsic to each dyad. Thus, the characteristic quality of interaction and attitude intrinsic to the husband-wife dyad is universally different from that of the father-son.

An organization of two or more dyads is a *structure*, as in the case of a nuclear family with parents and unmarried children, or in the case of a small store with one employer and several employees. An organization of attributes makes up a *content*. The content of a store and that of a nuclear family are obviously different, but even two nuclear families identical in structure may have different contents. For example, in one household the parents may act as though they each possess the children and have exclusive control over them, the father in competition with the mother for the affection of one or more of the children. This is an example of kinship content which is different from another kind in which the grandparents, whether they live in the same household with the parents or not, have a much greater say in the rearing of the children so that the parents do not have exclusive powers over them.

How are the dyads organized into a structure and attributes into a content? Here the concepts dominant dyad and dominant attribute come into play. Though a nuclear family consists of many dyads, usually one (sometimes two) enjoys a commanding position over the others. That dyad in this position is the *dominant dyad* and its requirements then take precedence over those of the others. For example, when the husband-wife dyad is dominant, the choice of mate, the residence pattern, divorce, rearing of minor children, and other decisions are likely to be in the hands of the man and his wife but not in the hands of his or her parents. If a man's wife does not get along with his mother, he is expected to take the side of his wife. Conversely, in a father-son-dominated structure all similar decisions are in the hands of the elders and disharmony between a man's mother and his wife may even constitute a legitimate ground for divorce.

The intrinsic attributes of a dominant dyad become the *dominant attributes* of the entire content. Thus, when the husband-wife dyad is dominant, the attributes of other dyads in that structure will be modified, and redefined, so as to conform to those of the dominant dyad, or even eliminated from the scene altogether. One of the universal attributes of the husband-wife dyad is sexuality, but if the father-son dyad is dominant, a man and his wife are expected to make no public expression of physical intimacy (such as kissing and hugging) at all. Conversely, if the husband-wife dyad is dominant, similar public expressions of physical intimacy will be required not only between marital partners but also between father and daughter and mother and son. However, kissing between father and son will not be in order because of the exaggerated fear of homosexuality, and a brother will be reluctant to go out with his sister (and vice versa) to avoid the suspicion that either is unable to attract anyone else.

The interrelationship among the various categories just explained are roughly represented in the following diagram:

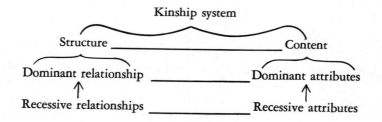

Having defined the terms, we are ready to tackle the hypothesis which, in skeletal form, is as follows: The dominant attributes of the dominant dyad in a given kinship system tend to determine the attitudes and action patterns which the individual in such a system develops toward other dyads in this system as well as toward his relationships outside of the system.

The reader can easily appreciate what this hypothesis attempts to do if he reflects on facts he already knows about food and nutrition. That food does something for the human body (in health or in sickness) is common knowledge. This fact was accepted long before we had any science of nutrition. *What precisely food does to what part of the human body, and how it works*, only gradually unfolds through research on nutrition. The latter translates food values into chemical elements such as protein and carbohydrates, or vitamins such as B_2 and C_1, and it is by means of this analysis and transformation that nutritionists enable us to see the links between specific foods and particular body requirements.

If we compare the kinship systems in our present hypothesis with different kinds of food, we can compare the adult attitudes and action patterns of a majority of individuals in different societies with body health and sickness. The dominant attributes in each kinship system are then comparable to the chemical elements or vitamins, which enable us to link a particular kind of kinship system with a particular variety of attitudes and action patterns in the society where that kinship system is found.

The parallels between the science of nutrition and our use of kinship can be made clear in the following diagramatical form:

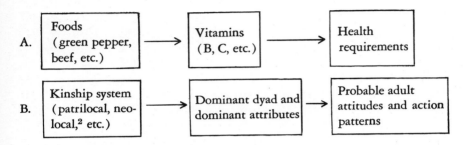

Without going into a detailed explication of this hypothesis, which can be found elsewhere (Hsu 1959, 1965, 1966a,b), we shall now briefly demonstrate how the hypothesis of dyadic dominance in kinship can help to link kinship with social and cultural behavior in the same two literate societies, namely, China and the United States, whose respective postulates we examined before.

According to this hypothesis (Hsu 1965), the Chinese kinship system is father-son dominated and its US counterpart is husband-wife dominated (hereafter designated F-S dominated and H-W dominated). The H-W-dominated kinship system is characterized by the following interrelated attributes: discontinuity, exclusiveness, sexuality, and volition; that of the F-S-dominated kinship system is dominated by the following interrelated attributes: continuity, inclusiveness, asexuality, and authority.

It is not possible to explain fully how the particular attributes flow from each of the two dyads. Briefly, the husband-wife dyad possesses the attribute of discontinuity because the husband-wife relationship is structurally independent of other dyads, for every husband is never a wife and every wife is never a husband (in science we sometimes have to elaborate the obvious in order to appreciate the not-so-obvious). There is no structural necessity for any husband-wife dyad, as such, to be connected with other husband-wife dyads as husband-wife dyads (this is in sharp contrast to the father-son dyad, shown below).

The husband-wife dyad exhibits exclusiveness because, while marriage in every society requires public recognition, every husband and wife must universally carry out by themselves alone some activities essential to the marital relationship. This remains true even where the custom is for one man to marry several

---

[2] Patrilocal residence is the custom whereby the wife lives under the roof of the husband's parents. Neolocal residence is the case when the newlyweds make a home of their own.

wives or one wife to marry several husbands. In the latter events the lone partner in the arrangement will fulfill his or her conjugal obligations with each of his or her spouses separately. The parties in a marriage everywhere share a degree of intimacy more intensive than those inherent in other relationships.

Sexuality is at the center of marital intimacy, which is the third attribute of the husband-wife dyad. And finally, the attribute of sexuality is the central reason why volition is another attribute of the husband-wife dyad. But in its widest extent, the attribute of volition characterizes the making of all marriages everywhere. Americans are generally aware of the fact that marriages in many other lands are not based on individual choice, but what needs to be pointed out is that even in such instances, there is always the question of choice—except that the volition of choice may be exercised by parents or other elders. However, over and above the question of choice of mate, sexuality involves a kind of need for individual willingness unknown or not required in the other relationships.

The attributes of the father-son dyad are in sharp contrast to those of the husband-wife dyad. The father-son relationship contains the attribute of continuity by virtue of the fact that every father is a son and every son in general is a father (or holds the promise of becoming one). Any father-son dyad is, therefore, a small link in a long chain of father-son dyads. The father-son dyad exhibits the attribute of inclusiveness because every father is not structurally tied to one son. In fact, every father holds the promise of having more than one child. The father-son relationship is inherently tolerant of other parties.

The link between the attribute of asexuality and the father-son dyad is obvious and needs no explanation. The connection between the attribute of authority and the father-son dyad comes from the basic fact that every father is older than the son (again I must ask leave of the reader for pointing out the obvious) and more powerful and experienced than the son, at least for a long period of time. Furthermore, it is rooted in a basic difference between men and women in every society. The role of men as men is that of having authority over women and children, as contrasted to that of women as women, which is responsibility for the care of children (Schneider 1961:6)[3]

Table 1 sets forth the kinds of behavior derivable from these attributes under four headings: (A) interpersonal relations, (B) institutional and cultural tendencies, (C) social organization, and (D) deviations or problems.

"Interpersonal relations" refers to the interactional patterns most likely to be desired by the individual or judged by him to be the most acceptable way of relating to his fellow men. "Institutional and cultural tendencies" consist of those behavioral characteristics which are most likely to support the relatively permanent features of the society and culture, or to influence them in given directions. "Social organization" consists of the ways human beings are linked together into different groups, for example, primary groups versus secondary groups, or kinship principle versus nonkinship principle, and the relative importance of one or another. "Deviations or problems" are those most likely to be

---

[3] For a discussion of how the various attributes of each dyad fit with each other see Hsu 1965: 644–645.

peculiar to each social organization. They are not deviations or problems in a universal sense, but occurrences which those concerned with the direction and maintenance of each society would like to eradicate or reduce. What may be considered deviations or problems in some societies may not be in other societies and cultures.

Under "behavior derivable" are given the kinds of probable behavior patterns most commensurate with the kinship dominance: H-W type or F-S type. For example, in a H-W-dominated kinship system a majority of individuals will tend to leave their parental homes and establish homes of their own, each containing a married couple and their unmarried children. This means the effective kinship group will forever remain small for all individuals. The way in which parents and children can get along best is as equals, not only after the youngster becomes an adult but even before. Yet some parents do not wish to grant independence to their children, or do not grant it in time, and this is one of the conditions productive of conflict between the generations. Conversely, some youngsters are too tied to the apron strings of their mothers (or unable to become psychological equals of their fathers). In such a society this becomes a serious matter of maladjustment.

Thus, the table will tell us that, for example, in the H-W-dominated kinship system the following behavior characteristics are derivable in the kinship sphere: The need for independence from parents and stress on equality with them are most commensurate behavior patterns in interpersonal relations; a high likelihood for rejection of parents is the most commensurate behavior pattern in institutional and cultural tendencies; the rule of monogamy and the proliferation of nonkinship groupings are most commensurate behavior patterns in social organization; conflict between the old and the young and attachment to father or mother, and so forth, are most likely to occur as deviations or problems. When the kinship system is that of an F-S-dominated one, then the behavior characteristics derivable will be found in the corresponding lower boxes in all instances.

The sample analysis given in Table 1, which translates the attributes of the contents of the F-S-dominated kinship system as contrasted to the H-W system, makes it obvious that some of the associations are testable by relatively objective means. For example, the extent to which the two peoples insist on independence or dependence in interpersonal relationships can easily be tested by interviewing sample groups of college students among both. Helen Codere's study of Vassar girls (1955, already cited) can easily be replicated among Chinese college girls in Taiwan or Hong Kong to reveal the extent to which the two groups differ in rejecting or retaining their kinship affiliation. It also can serve as a basis for corresponding and comparable analyses not only of other literate societies, such as Hindu India (Hsu 1963) and Japan (Hsu 1966b), but also of nonliterate societies.[4] Finally, it can also be shown that the behavior patterns derivable from the United States and Chinese kinship systems fully support their respective postulates, which we shall see below.

---

[4] The beginnings of a comparable analysis have been made by Fernandez on Zulu and Fang societies (1966) and by Howard on Rotuma and Fiji societies (1966).

TABLE 1
KINSHIP TYPE AND BEHAVIOR

Society and Culture	Kinship Type	Behavior Derivable	
		1. *Kinship*	2. *Maturity*
A. Interpersonal relations	1. H–W	Need for independence; stress on equality	Transformation of parent-child relationship to one of equals; finding self
	2. F–S	Need for dependence; stress on hierarchy	Finding one's place in the existing scheme of things and learning the proper roles
B. Institutional and cultural tendencies	1. H–W	Rejection (high)	Being different from parents; high impact of either parent or both on offspring
	2. F–S	Continuation (high)	Satisfaction with status quo; impact of parents mixed with that of ancestors and living kin
C. Social organization	1. H–W	Monogamy; proliferation of nonkinship groupings	Overwhelming importance of peer group
	2. F–S	Polygyny; clan organization	Overwhelming importance of kinship group; of performance of proper roles
D. Deviations or problems	1. H–W	Conflict between generations; continued attachment to mother or father; being orphaned, and so forth	Juvenile delinquency; inability to transform father-son relationship into brother-brother relationship; lack of initiative, dependence, and so forth
	2. F–S	Unfilialness; failure to keep father's status or family wealth; disharmony between mother-in-law, daughter-in-law, and so forth	Unfilialness; inability to exercise authority; no sons; ambition beyond custom; leaving home without family reason; lack of feeling of responsibility to close relatives

Behavior Derivable

3. Competition	4. House Patterns
Emphasis is on self; more pervasive, and so forth	Privacy important; children separate bedrooms when possible, and so forth
Emphasis on kinship group (for example, on help-brothers, and so forth); less pervasive	Privacy discouraged; senior persons live in best parts, and so forth
Formation of diverse groups for diverse objectives; (Catholic priests' call for union, February 23, 1966)	Houses with no walks around them; small and compact houses by desire, and so forth
Formation of large groups among nonkin difficult; less diverse objectives; size of groups small; and so forth	Houses with walls or other ways to separate them from each other; big houses with many generations under one roof wherever financially possible; separation of house into inner and outer parts.
Importance of entry or formation of nonkinship group as basis for	Houses with many internal and external signs of status; individual designs important, and so forth
Importance of kinship groups as basis for	External signs of status more important than internal ones; nonindividual designs; prestige conferred on greater expression of the conventional
Short cut against members in the same club	Busting or crashing of neighborhoods
Accentuation of nepotism; breakup of big family due to brother-brother and in-law tensions, and the like	House worth and style incommensurate with one's economic and social status

(continued)

TABLE 1 (*continued*)

Behavior Derivable

		5. Work (*Economics*)	6. Authority (*Politics*)
A	1	Employer-employee relationship impersonal; efficiency main criteria for hiring and firing; strikes common	Need for justification for obedience; authority is resented; need for image-building on part of leaders; leader-follower relationship personal
	2	Employer-employee relationship many-sided and personal; non-economic criteria for hiring and firing important; strikes uncommon, lack of attention to labor saving	No need to justify authority; authority not resented; impersonal relationship with leaders
B	1	Unions strong; organizing efforts relentless	Proliferation of laws; formation of large political action groups and tendency to fission; reduction of external signs of power
	2	Unions absent or weak and small; perfunctory	Few laws; large or small political groups tend to exist without much danger of fission; no need to reduce external signs of power
C	1	Big-business organizations common; tendency to centralization; peddlers scarce	Totalitarianism or democracy; objection to women in authority; positive involvement (support, reject, and so forth)
	2	Family business common; impersonal share-holding companies lacking or rare	Autocratic or local forms of government; women more easily achieve high place of authority; passive acquiescence
D	1	Proliferation and duplication of efforts; emphasis on change or induced obsolescence	Nonvoting citizens; indifference of citizens; subversion and suspicion of it; corruption
	2	Lack of innovation; internally developed efficiency low	Expression of dissatisfaction; rebellion; corruption

Behavior Derivable

7. Supernatural (Religion)	8. Values (Interpersonal Relations)
Monotheism, hostility toward other gods, priests, and believers, or attempt to convert them; God tends to be friendly, all good and equal with man	Self-reliance; superiority over others
Polytheism, indifference toward other gods, priests, and believers; will ask gods for favors when humans fail	Mutual dependence; respect for positions with emphasis that some are bound to be in low and others in high positions (the former must respect the latter)
Separatist groups of believers; close relation or rivalry between church and state (like incest taboo)	Proliferation of interest groups; from gourmet and nudist to preventing and promoting causes
Few or no separatist groups; politics and religion have little relation or conflict	Lack of enjoyment and cause-oriented groups
Highly organized "churches"; hierarchy of "churches"; proliferation of faiths	Higher degree of organicness in the society
Slightly organized, or unorganized "churches"; little hierarchy among "churches"; ancestor worship strong	Lower degree of organicness in the society
Division and fission among "churches" and believers; intermarriage among believers of different faiths; atheism	Mistreatment of children; oppression of women and others; lack of opportunity for same; protest movements, including violence
Neglect of ancestral rites; overzealousness about gods and spirits	Lack of food; lack of wise officials with integrity; violence

(*continued*)

TABLE 1 *(continued)*

Behavior Derivable

		9. Ideals (*Such as National Pronouncements, Great Books*)	10. *Approach to Sex*
A	1	Freedom, equality, and individual happiness; violence to reach them if necessary	Exaggeration and diffusion into most spheres of life; problem of masculinity versus femininity very pronounced
	2	Filial piety; respect for authority, age, and place; people should not be hungry and frustrated in sex	Relegation into small corner of life; little problem of masculinity versus femininity
B	1	Civil-rights movements; WCTU; moral rearmament; Black Muslims; KKK; violence for goals, and so forth	Pressure for equality of the sexes; pressure for naked expression of sex
	2	Public reward for filial piety; rich give charity to the poor; *Twenty-four Examples of Filial Piety*	Pressure toward reduction of expression of sex
C	1	Democracy or totalitarianism in terms of freedom and equality	Women seem to dominate; fear of women in high places
	2	Autocracy, benevolent despotism, and local and clan rule; education for the few; rule by the elite	Men seem to dominate, but no fear for women in high places
D	1	All obstacles to freedom, equality, and individual happiness	Frigidity in sex; maladjustment; fear of male homosexuality
	2	Starvation; corruption; immorality	Open expressions of sexual affection; looseness and infidelity in female

Behavior Derivable

11. *Literature* (*Novels*)	12. *Recreation*
Personal exploits of great heros in romance, adventure, conquest, or fight against injustice; romantic themes predominate; central focus: self	Action; need for active stimuli for relaxation; alcohol
Power of social and political structures; exploits of great men who are exceptionally moral, physically skillful, or high in supernatural accomplishment and who straightened out the injustices suffered by little men; central focus: man's place	Quietude, mild action; social visit without alcohol; action; inactive or active stimuli for relaxation
Protest against inequality and injustice; against restriction on sex; against inaction; men who explore the unbeaten path; triumph of romantic love against obstacles; finding self	Novel or dangerous games welcome; proliferation of new games and sports
Support for existing order; men urged to excel over others along the traditional path in morality, loyalty, and skill	Rejection of dangerous games; old games and pastimes retain popularity without much change
No novels in support of social organization; the glorification of conflict and triumph of the underdog; flight from reality	Team or individual games of victory and defeat; violence; gladiators to boxers; mountain climbing; collecting
Many novels in support of dynasties and law and order under the emperor; rise and fall of dynasties and families; satire on society through supernatural stories	Individual and occasionally team games, generally no absolute victory and defeat; cricket and rooster fights; chess; kicking feathercocks
Pornography and near pornography; novels that do not extol individual hearts and soul	Gambling; alcoholism; lack of playgrounds and other facilities
Novels that extol individual emotions and individual solutions to problems regardless of social order	Gambling to excess; excessive zeal for games and sports

Many more categories of "Behavior derivable" are obtainable besides this sample of twelve just given in the table. In attempting to delineate "Behavior derivable" it is necessary to keep in mind that most civilizations, literate or non-literate, are complex and that it will be difficult in the foreseeable future to link all its manifestations to its kinship system. In fact, I am not sure that all aspects of a civilization are functionally linkable to its kinship system. What I am quite sure of, however, is that a substantial part (in fact, the central part) of each civilization must be related to its kinship system. Furthrmore, I am also sure that this relationship between the central part of each civilization and its kinship system can be effectively and systematically demonstrated as we develop more efficient conceptual tools. These tools should enable us more and more to translate the forces operating in the kinship sector into meaningful entities for understanding what goes on in the larger society and culture. With the new concepts introduced here (content, dominant dyad, attribute, and dominant attribute) I have made a beginning. What I hope to see is more students taking up the challenge.

I shall conclude this chapter by outlining what I consider the central part of each civilization which may be linked with kinship and which may serve as an effective basis for comparison among all kinds of societies, literate and nonliterate. The following is an adequate but not exhaustive list:

I. Attitudes: Toward self, maturity, authority, sex, illness, the supernatural and life after death, obligation, honors, competition, conflict (both cognitive and evaluative)

II. Basic relationships: Kinship, gift making, friendship, association, religious grouping, local government (including arrangements for the maintenance of law and order), bureaucracy, property ownership and trading, inheritance (all relationships to be examined in terms of content versus structure)

III. Material elements: Clothing, house patterns (within each house, and relationship between different houses), layout of town or village, special features such as wells, level of technology

IV. Work: Basic ways of making a living; work organization; employment relationship; relationship among producers, middlemen, and consumers, or between any two or them

V. Projective culture: Art, literature, folklore, myths, values, ideals (as reflections of the psychic materials that are shared among a majority of people; must have statements as to their popularity or durability)

VI. Recreational activities: Games, contests, festivals, pageantry, holiday activities

10

Final Observations

BESIDES THE APPROACHES DISCUSSED in the last two chapters for studying literate civilizations (and for making such studies relevant to those primarily keyed to nonliterate societies), there are obviously other possibilities. One approach is that of Whiting and associates, who single out certain variables from many different cultures for meaningful correlations. Their work has so far primarily been centered in nonliterate societies, but, since the variables dealt with are few and well-defined, their approach can easily be used to explore literate civilizations as well. In an extensive review of the cross-cultural data Whiting has supplied us with the following typology of the different ways that "personality can serve as a mediator between the maintenance and projective systems of a culture."

The most common type is shown in Figure 1. Here it is assumed that a certain feature of maintenance systems determines a child-training practice and that this practice determines a feature in the projective systems, but that the given feature of the maintenance systems has no directly determining influence with respect to the projective system feature. This type can be illustrated by the relation between household structure, infant indulgence, and the nature of the gods as described above: that is, extended family households predict high infant indulgence, and high infant indulgence predicts a low fear of ghosts, but household structure is unrelated to the fear of ghosts.

Figure 1. The mediation type.

Another important type is shown in Figure 2. Here it is assumed that neither a feature of the maintenance system nor a child-rearing practice alone will determine a given feature in the projective system but that taken together they will. As an example, the age of weaning predicts guilt in monogamous but not polygynous societies.

Figure 2.   The interaction type.

It is more likely that many more examples of this type will be discovered as research in this area becomes more sophisticated.

The third type, shown in Figure 3, assumes a direct effect of pressures from the maintenance system upon some aspect of the projective system.

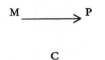

Figure 3.   Adult pressure type.

Although this type was not considered in this review, a recent study showing heavy drinking to be associated with bilateral descent, but to none of the child-rearing variables discussed above, is a good example of this type.

Figure 4 indicates the assumption of causation between a child-rearing and a projective feature in a direction opposite to that which has usually been assumed in the

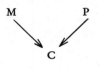

Figure 4.   "Reverse" causation.

studies under review. The only case of this type noted is from the study by Lambert and his group where training in self-reliance and independence was interpreted as being a consequence rather than the cause of a belief in aggressive gods (Whiting 1961:376–377).

The usual objection to this and other Whiting exercises is that they involve enormous assumptive jumps between the correlates that are not substantially bridged. It seems that this objection can be met by using the correlations obtained through his method as leads in more extensive ethnographic exploration (in the library or the field) for specific evidence in their support or refutation in some of the behavior categories we gave in Chapter 9.

For example, Whiting and co-workers postulated, with some justification, that exclusive mother-infant sleeping arrangements are strongly associated with severe male initiation rites at puberty because such sleeping arrangements (1) increased the Oedipal rivalry between son and father and that initiation rites served to prevent open and violent revolt against parental authority at a time when physical maturity would make such revolt dangerous and socially disruptive, (2) led to excessively strong dependence upon the mother which initiation rites served to break, and (3) produced strong identification with the mother which the rites served to counteract (Whiting *et al.* 1958:359–370). Can we not examine the context of each case by searching for evidence in support or refutation of the prominence of mother-infant exclusiveness or father-son hostility or mother-son attachment not only through the sleeping arrangements (which come under our category III material elements) but also in attitudes, basic relationship, and so forth?

In each society with mother-infant exclusive sleeping arrangements we must see if the sleeping arrangements are the only area of mother-infant exclusiveness and therefore are, in related areas, *counterbalanced* by nonexclusiveness, or are *reinforced* also by more exclusiveness. Furthermore, even if the mother-infant exclusiveness is reinforced in related areas by more exclusiveness (in which case we may reasonably expect the mother-infant exclusive sleeping arrangements to have a more massive imprint than otherwise on the personality of the youth), the prevailing attitudes in the civilization toward dependency and toward masculinity and femininity in general will obviously have an important bearing on the outcome. That is to say, if mother-infant exclusive sleeping arrangement is reinforced in other areas of life of the society by more mother-child exclusiveness, we shall have good grounds for anticipating the need for severe male initiation rites at puberty to break and counteract, respectively, the dependence upon, and the identification with, the mother, but if the society has no negative evaluation of dependency and of covert or overt femininity in males, then there is no need for severe initiation rites to break the dependence upon the mother or to counteract the identification with her.

The latter analysis fits the case of Hindu India, where there is "maximum conflict in sex identity, e.g., where a boy initially sleeps exclusively with his mother and where the domestic unit is patrilocal and hence controlled by men" (Burton and Whiting 1960:90), but where, according to my observations, neither dependency nor femininity in males are negative values or problems for the individual (Hsu 1963, 1965). In such an event we anticipate no need for severe initiation rites for males. There are, indeed, no initiation rites in Hindu India except the donning of the sacred thread at puberty or before.

The initiation rites in Whiting's studies predominantly comprise hazing, genital mutilation, seclusion from women, and tests of endurance. There is nothing like them connected with puberty in Hindu India. The sacred thread rite has no trace of overt sex symbolism and is primarily restricted to Brahmins (or all caste Hindus, meaning those who fit some criteria of being Brahmins, Kshatryas, and Vaishyas) and is only occasionally extended to lower castes such as the Pancha Brahma of Shamirpet, Hyderabad, Kayastha of Bengal, or (in modified form) the Lingayat of Deccan, for caste-raising purposes. Yet observational and projective data indicate that Hindu males would seem to exhibit a high degree of dependency as well as uncertainty of sex identity. Presuming Whiting's hypothesis to be correct, our inference is that this seeming uncertainty is more of a problem to the outside observer than to the Hindu. The fact that a majority of Hindu males undergo no initiation rite, and that those who do regard it primarily as a matter of caste status, is an important evidence in support of our inference.[1]

So far most psychological anthropologists, including myself, have made use of the concept of basic personality, social personality, or just personality in our discussion of the interrelationship among individual, society, and culture. Some scholars have detected a danger of reification in such concepts and developed something that might eventually be termed "cognitive anthropology" (at present generally known as "ethnoscience")[2] with central emphasis on exhaustive sum total of knowledge in any given area. To the extent that they will try to achieve some sort of integration of language, culture, cognition, and behavior, they may succeed in bypassing any concept of personality. Or by studying the quantity and, more importantly, the quality and style of application of individual knowledges selected from the pool of the sum total of available knowledge in a given culture, they may at least give the concept of personality a more precise meaning. Some representative works in this direction are found in three collections (Romney and D'Andrade 1964; Gumperz and Hymes 1964; Hymes 1964).

Quite naturally the central focus of these works is the relationship between language and culture: (1) the universality of a semantic framework underlying (a) lexical structure as reflected by folk taxonomies in the broadest sense of the term [for example, kinship in the works of Lounsbury (1964) and Goodenough (1955); color categories and investigations of taxonomies in the works of Conklin (1962), Wallace and Atkins (1960), and Werner (in press); medicine and other domains in the work of Frake (1962a and 1962b), Metzger and Williams (1963a, 1963b); and many others] and (b) certain affective or connotative aspects of all languages (for example, in spite of culture differences all languages seem to share the three reactive dimensions of evaluation, such as good-bad, potency such as strong-weak, and activity such as fast-slow (Osgood 1964: 171–200); (2) the cultural differences in mathematical concept learning (for example, American and Ghanaian children share the same learning curve with reference to identity of sets, though they differ in other respects (Hill 1964:201–222); or (3) the phonological and grammatical similarities of baby talk across linguistic barriers (Ferguson 1964:102–114).

---

[1] Whiting's hypothesis on initiation rites has recently been challenged by Yehudi Cohen (1964), whose grounds for the challenge do not, however, eliminate the possibility that initiation rites may be at least partially related to the problem of sex identity in many societies. However, the Hindu rite connected with the donning of the sacred thread obviously is consonant with Cohen's idea of the need for the society to manipulate "the child in relation to the boundaries of his nuclear family and kin group in order to implant a social emotional identity and values consonant with the culture's articulating principles." In the Hindu case the boundary is that of caste instead of kin group and the principle underlying it is hierarchy. For a more thorough investigation of the entire subject of initiation ceremonies with many new methodological innovations and insight, see Young 1965.

[2] The essence of what ethnoscience students are doing can be found in all first-rate ethnographies such as those of Malinowski, Evans-Pritchard, and Firth. The difference is that whereas the excellent field results before ethnoscience were dependent upon the virtuosity of individual fieldworkers, the group of scholars interested in ethnoscience have made it more possible for the required skill to be more expressly discussed and taught to a larger number of prospective students. Though the term "ethnoscience" is not fully justified and is in some ways a misnomer, and though some may see it as an attention-getting device for a kind of work that ethnographers have always been doing anyway, the positive effect of this development will be to raise the standard and comparability of ethnography in general.

These endeavors hold at least two basic implications for the study of man. First, their data are drawn from different societies without reference to the literate versus nonliterate barrier and are broadly interdisciplinary. Pure linguistic researches have for long disregarded the distinction between literate and nonliterate languages, but now it is shown that this can also be effectively done in the study of languages in relation to cultures. Second, and this is a much more untrodden path, they attempt to elucidate perceptual categories by different "levels of contrast" (for example, Conklin 1964:189–192 and Frake 1964:193–211). For example, Conklin shows that color distinctions in Hanunóo, a tribe in the Philippines, are made "at two levels of contrast, one being more general than the other. The first, higher, more general level consists of an all-inclusive, coordinate, four-way classification which lies at the core of the color system":

1. Relative darkness (of shade of color); blackness (black)
2. Relative lightness (or tint of color); whiteness (white)
3. Relative presence of red; redness (red)
4. Relative presence of light greenness; greenness (green) (Conklin 1964:190)

Frake does a similar but more comprehensive analysis of the more difficult matter of diagnosis of disease among the Subanun of Mindanao by eliciting and analyzing different diagnostic criteria through contrasts and levels (Frake 1964: 193–205). The details need not occupy us here, but the importance of the methodology they and others engaged in this line of inquiry have initiated promises a day when subjects more complicated than color perception or disease diagnosis may be similarly treated. We shall have made enormous scientific advances when we can with the same precision ascertain the levels of contrast in authority, in devotion to the supernatural, in marital harmony, or in kinship nearness and distance.

However, even when we have successfully tackled some of the more complex aspects of society and civilization by ethnoscience techniques, we may still be a long way from eliminating the term "personality," with or without qualifiers, in psychological anthropology. The situation may be compared with the present scientific status of the concepts of family, clan, culture, society, and even tribe. For example, seeing that the Nuer mean by "family" a very different entity from what the Tallensi mean by it, some students have questioned the wisdom of the continued use of the term. So we have added a whole series of qualifiers to the term family: "nuclear family," "biological family," or "matricentric family"; or have avoided the term altogether by such terminological devices as "domestic group," "domestic unit," or "patrilocal household." These new additions or modifications have not, however, negated the fact that the concept of family has continued to serve as a sort of convenient handle to designate a complex of human relationships centered in marriage and parenthood.

Besides, overreliance on ethnoscience techniques will lead us to the same difficulties as that on ethnographically derived criteria for comparison with reference to theory building—a point we discussed before. What these more precise techniques can do for us is to gather more complete and more precise knowledge of many a single culture. What they may also do is to prevent us from seeing the forest for the trees. Massive factual details can help us to verify or disprove a theory, but theories never emerge out of massive factual details. The relationship between facts is the essence of theory, which can only be deductively arrived at in the first place. The concepts of personality, family, clan, and so forth, on which our present theories hang may be under attack. The only scientifically acceptable rationale for dropping them will be the fact that we have found more efficient concepts with which to marshal our factual details, but not that we shall have no need for them or other concepts.

Finally, the attack on all of these terms may have evoked in the minds of some readers the idea that perhaps the scientific usefulness of the concept of national character is also in doubt. This concept has been under attack from diverse quarters, sometimes with good reason. There is no question but that as Americans acquire more specific knowledge about Germans (or any people A with reference to any people B), they may see many patterns of behavior exhibited by the Germans as not peculiar to Germans but common to all men (as against all women), to all teen-agers (as against all adults), to all employers (as against all employees), and the like, across national or cultural boundaries. The classical Marxian view that economic interests will unite workers in different societies has been severely challenged by modern-day nationalistic divisions among nations governed by socialism. Even the more scientific formulation of Alex Inkeles, backed by extensive field interviews, does not permit us, now or in the foreseeable future, to discard the concept of national character (much less the safer concepts of nation or national culture) as indicating an important way of understanding the psychological basis of interpersonal or intersocietal behavior.

Inkeles' study of the relation of industrial man in a variety of countries from the United States, the Soviet Union, and Germany to Italy, Mexico, and Australia is aimed at demonstrating his proposition

> that men's environment, as expressed in the institutional patterns they adopt or have introduced to them, shapes their experience, and through this their perceptions, attitudes and values, in standardized ways which are manifest from country to country, despite the countervailing randomizing influence of traditional cultural patterns (Inkeles 1960:2).

What Inkeles has dealt with are limited aspects of life and opinions: job satisfaction by occupation, quality most desired in a work situation, economic superiority and self-admitted happiness, belief in the possibility of change in human nature by country and class, and so forth. Even so, the results do not converge in the same direction. For example, while the estimates of job security among different occupational groups are similar from country to country, those of personal economic betterment exhibit no comparable consistency in pattern (Inkeles 1960:25–28). In Japan, however, the families of "salarymen" and "small businessmen" alike sleep in clusters of parents and children. Economic status differences do not separate them from a basically Japanese arrangement which has many implications in Japanese character (Caudill and Plath 1966). Furthermore, it should be noted that all data included in the Inkeles survey, except for a small Japanese sample, were obtained from Western societies. They provide us, therefore, essentially, with the Western industrial men's views of the issues concerned rather than those of industrial men across cultural boundaries.[3] However, this does not negate the fact that within a large cultural area common economic structures and life experiences may produce similar responses in different subcultures. Here Inkeles has merely substituted the factory for particular customs in the household (a central concern of Whiting and colleagues) or peculiarities in kinship content (by way of my concept of dominant dyads). He does not challenge culture as an influence and source of variation.

We must recognize two things. First, there are scientifically acceptable and scientifically unacceptable national character studies. I have examined some of these. The interested reader will find a comprehensive survey by Inkeles and Levinson (1968) most useful. We cannot throw away the baby with the bath water.

Second, it seems that the whole is more than the sum of its parts. We have to date achieved a very advanced anatomical and physiological understanding of the human body, but we have yet to unlock for certain the secret of what makes life or to refute the still-accepted theory of biogenesis—that each living organism, however simple, arises by some reproductive process (budding, fission, spore formation, or sexual reproduction) from a parent organism. What we have today in national character studies, as well as in personality and culture studies, are more clearly and minutely identified differences in value orientation, in institutions and groupings, and in the way or ways most individuals seem to function in them. Such differences are identified through cultural postulates or patterns of kinship. We have by no means the assurance that, having perceived these differences in value orientation, institutions and grouping, and individual functioning, we now know what makes Americans American, or Frenchmen French. What we do claim is merely that knowing those differences will enable us to understand their respective social and cultural developments better than if we did not.

We must continue to explore the similarities in different societies and civilizations, but we will not have served our discipline well by premature replacement of one kind of terminology for another kind, especially if, in doing so, we run the danger of neglecting the intersocietal and intercivilizational differences.

---

[3] Lack of comparable materials obviously made the latter type of comparison impractical, but the implications of Inkeles' conclusions should not be extended beyond what his data warrant.

References

ADAMS, G. F., and E. A. CHEESEMAN, 1951, *Old People in Northern Ireland*. Belfast: Northern Ireland Hospitals Authority.

ADAMS, RICHARD N., 1959, *A Community in the Andes: Problems and Progress in Muquiyauyo*. Seattle: University of Washington Press.

ADORNO, T. W., E. FRENKEL-BRUNSWIK, M. J. LEVINSON, and F. SUTTON, 1950, *The Authoritarian Personality*. New York: Harper & Row.

Africa, October 1935, 8, 4.

ALBERT, ETHEL M., 1963a, Conflict and Change in American Values: A Culture-Historical Approach. *Ethics* 74:19–33.

———, 1963b, Value Aspects of Teaching Anthropology. In *The Teaching of Anthropology*, D. G. Mandelbaum, G. W. Lasker, and E. M. Albert (eds.). AAA Memoir 94:559–581.

AMMAR, HAMED, 1954, *Growing Up in an Egyptian Village*. London: Routledge.

ANDERSON, ROBERT T., and BARBARA G. ANDERSON, 1965, *Bus Stop for Paris: The Transformation of a French Village*. Garden City, N.Y.: Doubleday.

ANDERSON, ROBERT T., and BARBARA GALLATIN, 1964, *The Vanishing Village: A Danish Maritime Community*. Seattle: University of Washington Press.

ARENSBERG, CONRAD M., 1937, *The Irish Countryman*. New York: Macmillan.

———, 1955, American Communities. *American Anthropologist* 57:1143–1162.

ARENSBERG, CONRAD M., and S. T. KIMBALL, 1948, *Family and Community in Ireland*. Cambridge: Harvard University Press.

———, 1965, *Culture and Community*. New York: Harcourt.

ARYOUT, HENRY HABIB, 1963, *The Egyptian Peasant*. John A. Williams, (tr.). Boston: Beacon.

ASTON, WILLIAM G., 1905, *Shinto: The Way of the Gods*. London: Longmans.

BAILEY, F. G., 1957, *Caste and the Economic Frontier: A Village in Highland Orissa*. Manchester: Manchester University Press.

BANFIELD, EDWARD C., 1958, *The Moral Basis of a Backward Society*. New York: Free Press.

BARNETT, CHARLES R., 1958, *Poland*. New Haven, Conn.: Human Relations Area Files, Survey of World Cultures.

BARTH, FREDRIK (ed.), 1963, *The Role of the Entrepreneur in Social Change in Northern Norway*. Bergen: Norwegian Universities Press.

BATESON, GREGORY, 1942, Some Systematic Approaches to the Study of Culture and Personality. *Character and Personality* 11:76–82, reproduced in *Personal Character and Social Milieu*, D. Haring (ed.). Syracuse, N.Y.: Syracuse University Press.

BAUER, RAYMOND, ALEX INKELES, and CLYDE KLUCKHOHN, 1956, *How the Soviet System Works: Cultural, Psychological and Social Themes*. Cambridge, Mass.: Harvard University Press.

BEALS, ALAN, 1962, *Gopalpur: A South Indian Village*. New York: Holt, Rinehart and Winston, Inc.

BEALS, RALPH L., and HARRY HOIJER, 1965, *An Introduction to Anthropology*. New York: Macmillan.

BEARDSLEY, RICHARD K., 1959, *Field Guide to Japan*. Washington, D.C.: Academy of Sciences, National Research Council.

BEARDSLEY, RICHARD K., JOHN W. HALL, and ROBERT E. WARD, 1959, *Village Japan.* Chicago: University of Chicago Press.

BENEDICT, RUTH, 1934, *Patterns of Culture.* New York: New American Library.

———, 1946, *The Chrysanthemum and the Sword.* Boston: Houghton Mifflin.

BENNETT, JOHN W., and MICHIO NAGAI, 1953, Echoes: Reactions to American Anthropology. (Japanese critique of the methodology of Benedict's *Chrysanthemum and the Sword.*) *American Anthropologist* 55:404–411.

BERREMAN, GERALD D., 1963, *Hindus of the Himalayas.* Berkeley. Calif.: University of California Press.

BLUM, RICHARD, and EVA BLUM, 1965, *Health and Healing in Greece: A Study of Three Communities.* Stanford, Calif.: Stanford University Press.

BOAS, FRANZ, 1896, The Limitations of the Comparative Method of Anthropology. Paper read at the meeting of A.A.A.S. at Buffalo, N.Y. *Science* 4:103:901–908.

BOHANNAN, PAUL J., 1960, *African Homicide and Suicide.* Princeton, N.J.: Princeton University Press.

———, 1967, Review of Max Gluckman's *The Ideas in Barotse Jurisprudence.* The Kroeber Anthropological Society Papers, No. 36. Berkeley, Calif.: Kroeber Anthropological Society.

BOOTH, CHARLES, 1902, *Life and Labour of the People in London.* 17 vols. London: Macmillan.

BRICKNER, R., 1943, *Is Germany Incurable?* Philadelphia: Lippincott.

BROGAN, D. W., 1944, *The American Character.* New York: Knopf.

BROWNE, C. R., 1929, *Maori Witchery.* London: Dent.

BURTON, ROGER V., and J. W. M. WHITING, 1960, The Absent Father: Effects on the Developing Child. Paper presented at A.P.A. Meeting, September.

CAMPBELL, J. K., 1964, *Honor, Family and Patronage: A Study of Institutions and Moral Values in a Greek Mountain Community.* London: Oxford.

CANNON, WALTER B., 1942, Voodoo Death. *American Anthropologist* 44:169–181.

CARSTAIRS, G. MORRIS, 1957, *The Twice Born.* London: Hogarth.

CAUDILL, WILLIAM, 1952, *Japanese-American Personality and Acculturation.* Provincetown, Mass.: Genetic Psychology Monograph 45.

———, 1958, *The Psychiatric Hospital as a Small Society.* Cambridge, Mass.: Harvard University Press.

———, 1959, Similarities and Differences in Psychiatric Illness and Its Treatment in the United States and Japan. Nagoya University, *Seishin Eisei (Mental Hygiene)* 61/62: 15–26.

CAUDILL, WILLIAM, and GEORGE DeVos, 1956, Achievement, Culture and Personality: The Case of the Japanese-Americans. *American Anthropologist* 58:1102–1127.

CAUDILL, WILLIAM, and DAVID W. PLATH, 1966, Who Sleeps by Whom? Parent-Child Involvement in Urban Japanese Families. *Psychiatry* 29:4:344–366.

CLARK, MARGARET, and BARBARA GALLATIN ANDERSON, 1967, *Culture and Aging.* Springfield, Ill.: Charles C Thomas.

CODERE, HELEN, 1955, A Genealogical Study of Kinship in the United States. *Psychiatry* 18:65–79.

COHEN, RONALD, 1967, *The Kanuri of Bornu.* New York: Holt, Rinehart and Winston, Inc.

COHEN, YEHUDI A., 1961, Food and Its Vicissitudes: A Cross-Cultural Study of Sharing and Non-sharing. In *Social Structure and Personality,* Yehudi A. Cohen (ed.). Based on 1955 essay. New York: Holt, Rinehart and Winston, Inc.

———, 1964, The Establishment of Identity in a Social Nexus: The Special Case of Initiation Ceremonies and Their Relation to Value and Legal Systems. *American Anthropologist* 66:529–552.

COHN, BERNARD S., 1961, The Pasts of an Indian Village. *Comparative Studies in Society and History,* 2, 3:248–249. The Hague: Mouton and Company.

COMMAGER, HENRY STEELE, 1950, *The American Mind.* New Haven: Yale University Press.

CONKLIN, HAROLD C., 1962, Lexicographical Treatment of Folk Taxonomies. In *Problems in Lexicography,* Fred W. Householder and Sol Saporta (eds.). Bloomington, Ind.: Indiana University Press, pp. 119–141.

——, 1964, Hanunóo Color Categories. In *Language in Culture and Society,* Dell Hymes (ed.). New York, Evanston, and London: Harper & Row.

CROOK, ISABEL and DAVID, 1966, *The First Years of Yangyi Commune.* New York: Humanities Press, Inc.

DAVIS, ALLISON, and JOHN DOLLARD, 1940, *Children of Bondage.* Washington, D.C.: American Council on Education.

DENNIS, N., F. HENRIQUES, and C. SLAUGHTER, 1956, *Coal is Our Life.* London: Eyre and Spottiswoode.

DESPRES, LEO A., 1966, Anthropological Theory, Cultural Pluralism and the Study of Complex Societies. Paper presented at the Conference on Anthropology and the Study of Complex Societies, Washington University, St. Louis. To be published in *Current Anthropology 1968.*

DE TOCQUEVILLE, ALEXIS, 1945, *Democracy in America.* Based on 1862 Bowen translation. New York: Knopf.

DEVOS, GEORGE, 1960a, The Relation of Guilt toward Parents to Achievement and Arranged Marriage among the Japanese. *Psychiatry: Journal for the Study of Interpersonal Processes,* 23, 3.

——, 1960b, Psycho-cultural Attitudes toward Primary Relationships in Japanese Delinquents—a Study in Progress. *Seishin Eisci (Mental Hygiene),* 66.

——, 1965, Achievement Orientation, Social Self-Identity, and Japanese Income Growth. *Asian Studies* 5:575.

DEVOS, GEORGE, and H. WAGATSUMA, 1959, Psychocultural Significance of Concern Over Death and Illness Among Rural Japanese. *International Journal of Social Psychiatry* 5:5–19.

——, 1961, Value Attitudes toward Role Behavior of Women in Two Japanese Villages. *American Anthropologist* 63:1204–1230.

DICKS, HENRY V., 1950, Personality Traits and National Socialist Ideology, a War-Time Study of German Prisoners of War. *Human Relations* 3:111–154.

DOI, TAKEO, 1958, *Shinkeishitsu no seishinbyori* (psychopathology of 'shinkeishitsu'). *Seishinshinkeigaku Zasshi (Psychiatria et Neurologia Japonica)* 60:733–44 (English abstract).

DOLLARD, JOHN, 1957, *Caste and Class in a Southern Town.* New York: Doubleday Anchor Books. (First published 1937. New Haven, Conn.: Yale University Press.)

DORE, RONALD P., 1958, *City Life in Japan.* Berkeley, Calif.: University of California Press.

DUBE, S. C., 1955, *Indian Village.* Ithaca, N.Y.: Cornell University Press.

DUBOIS, CORA, 1944, *The People of Alor.* New York: Harper & Row.

DUIJKER, H. C. F., and N. M. FRIJDA, 1961, *National Character and National Stereotypes: A Trend Report Prepared for the International Union of Scientific Psychology.* New York: Humanities Press, Inc.

DUMONT, LOUIS, and D. POCOCK, 1958, *Contributions to Indian Sociology.* Paris and The Hague: Mouton and Company, an irregular publication, No. 2:49.

DUNN, STEPHEN P., and ETHEL DUNN, 1967, *The Peasants of Central Russia,* New York: Holt, Rinehart and Winston, Inc.

EBERHARD, WOLFRAM, 1952, *Chinese Festivals.* New York: Abelard-Schuman.

EGGAN, FRED, 1954, Social Anthropology and the Method of Controlled Comparison. *American Anthropologist* 56:5:743–763.

EGLAR, ZEKIYE, 1960, *A Punjab Village in Pakistan.* New York: Columbia University Press.

ELISSÉEFF, SERGE, 1963, The Mythology of Japan. In *Asiatic Mythology* by Hachin and associates. Translated from the French, 1928. New York: Crowell. pp. 385–448.

EMBREE, JOHN, 1939, *Suye Mura, A Japanese Village*. Chicago: University of Chicago Press.

ERIKSON, ERIK H., 1963, *Childhood and Society*. 2d ed. revised. First ed., 1950. New York: Norton.

ERSKINE, WILLIAM H., 1933, *Japanese Festival and Calendar Lore*. Tokyo: Kyo bun-kwan.

EVANS-PRITCHARD, E. E., 1937, *Witchcraft, Oracles and Magic among the Azande*. London: Oxford.

FARBER, MAURICE L., 1950, The Problem of National Character: A Methodological Analysis. *Journal of Psychology* 30:307–316.

———, 1951, English and Americans: A Study in National Character. *Journal of Psychology* 32:241–249.

FEI, H. T., 1939, *Peasant Life in China: A Field Study of Country Life in the Yangtze Valley*. London: Routledge.

FEI, H. T., and C. I. CHANG, 1945, *Earthbound China*. Chicago: University of Chicago Press.

FERGUSON, CHARLES A., 1964, Diglossia. In *Language in Culture and Society*, Dell Hymes (ed.). A Reader in Linguistics and Anthropology. New York: Harper & Row.

FERNANDEZ, JAMES W., 1966, Bantu Brotherhood. The Compatability of the Hsu Hypothesis with Some Bantu Materials. Paper prepared for participation in Wenner-Gren Foundation for Anthropological Research Symposium on "Kinship and Culture," August 20–29. To be included in *Kinship and Culture*, in preparation. Edited by Hsu.

FIRTH, RAYMOND, 1954, The Sociology of "Magic" in Tikopia. *Sociologus*, 14, New Series: 103, 113–115

FIRTH, RAYMOND (ed.), 1956, *Two Studies of Kinship in London*. London: The Athlone Press.

FORDE, DARYLL, and MARY DOUGLAS FORDE, 1956, Primitive Economics. In *Man, Culture and Society*, Harry L. Shapiro (ed.). New York: Oxford, pp. 330–344.

Fortune, 1940, 21, 2:14ff.

FOSTER, GEORGE M., 1948, *Empire's Children: The People of Tzintzuntzan*. Washington, D.C.: Smithsonian Institution, Publication No. 16.

———, 1953, What is Folk Culture? *American Anthropologist* 55:159–173.

———, 1965, Peasant Society and the Image of the Limited Good. *American Anthropologist* 67:293–315.

———, 1967, *Tzintzuntzan: Mexican Peasants in a Changing World*. Boston: Little, Brown.

FRAKE, CHARLES O., 1962a, The Ethnographic Study of Cognitive Systems. In *Anthropology and Human Behavior*, Thomas Gladwin and William C. Sturtevant (eds.). Washington, D.C.: Anthropological Society of Washington.

———, 1962b, Cultural Ecology and Ethnography. *American Anthropologist* 64:53–59.

———, 1964, The Diagnosis of Disease Among the Subanun of Mindanao. In *Language in Culture and Society*, Dell Hymes (ed.). New York: Harper & Row, pp. 193–211.

FRANKENBERG, RONALD, 1957, *Village on the Border: A Social Study of Religion, Politics and Football in a North Wales Community*. London: Cohen and West.

FRASER, THOMAS M., JR., 1966, *Fishermen of South Thailand: The Malay Villagers*. New York: Holt, Rinehart and Winston, Inc.

FRAZIER, EDWARD F., 1939, *The Negro Family in the United States*. Chicago: University of Chicago Press.

———, 1940, *Negro Youth at the Crossways*. Washington, D.C.: American Council on Education.

FRIED, MORTON H., 1953, *Fabric of Chinese Society*. New York: Praeger.

FRIEDL, ERNESTINE, 1962, *Vasilika: A Village in Modern Greece*. New York: Holt, Rinehart and Winston, Inc.

FRIEDMANN, FREDRICK G., 1960, *The Hoe and the Book: An Italian Experiment in Community Development*. Ithaca: Cornell University Press.

FRIEDRICH, PAUL, 1964, Semantic Structure and Social Structure: An Instance from Russian. In *Explorations in Cultural Anthropology*, Ward H. Goodenough (ed.). New York: McGraw-Hill.

FROMM, ERICH, 1941, *Escape from Freedom*. New York: Farrar, Straus.

FULLER, ANNE H., 1961, *Burarij: Portrait of a Lebanese Muslim Village*. Cambridge: Harvard University Press.

GALLAHER, ART, 1961, *Plainville Fifteen Years Later*. New York: Columbia University Press.

GALLIN, BERNARD, 1966, *Hsin Hsing, Taiwan: A Chinese Village in Change*. Berkeley and Los Angeles: University of California Press.

GAMBLE, SIDNEY D., 1954, *Ting Hsien, A North China Rural Community*. New York: International Secretariat, Institute of Pacific Relations.

———, 1963, *North China Villages: Social, Political and Economic Activities before 1933*. Berkeley: University of California Press.

GAMIO, MANUEL, 1922, *La Poblacion del Valle de San Juan Teotihuacan*. Mexico.

GEDDES, ARTHUR, 1955, *The Isle of Lewis and Harris: A Study in British Community*. Edinburgh: Edinburgh University Press.

GEERTZ, CLIFFORD, 1960, *The Religion of Java*. New York: Free Press.

GILLESPIE, JAMES M., and GORDON W. ALLPORT, 1955, *Youth's Outlook on the Future: A Cross National Study*. New York: Doubleday.

GILLIN, JOHN P., 1951, *The Culture of Security in San Carlos*. Pub. No. 16. New Orleans Tulane University of Louisiana Middle American Research Institute.

GLUCKMAN, MAX, 1965, *The Ideas of Barotse Jurisprudence*. New Haven: Yale University Press.

GOLDSCHMIDT, WALTER, 1947, *As You Sow*. New York: Harcourt.

———, 1950, Social Class in America—A Critical Review. *American Anthropologist* 52:483–498.

GOODE, WILLIAM J., 1963, *World Revolution and Family Patterns*. New York: Free Press.

GOODENOUGH, WARD H., 1955, A Problem in Malayo-Polynesian Social Organization. *American Anthropologist* 57:71–83.

———, 1965, Yankee Kinship Terminology: A problem in componental analysis. *American Anthropologist* 67, 2:259–287.

GORER, GEOFFREY, 1948, *The American People* (Revised edition in 1964). New York: Norton.

———, 1955, *Exploring English Character*. London: The Cresset Press.

GORER, GEOFFREY, and JOHN RICKMAN, 1962, *The People of 'Great Russia*. Reprinted. New York: Chanticleer Press.

GULICK, JOHN, 1955, *Social Structure and Culture Change in a Lebanese Village*. Viking Fund Publications in Anthropology, No. 21. New York.

GUMPERZ, JOHN J., and DELL HYMES (eds.), 1964, The Ethnography of Communication. *American Anthropologist* Special Publication, Vol. 66.

HALL, EDWARD T., 1966, *The Hidden Dimension*. New York: Doubleday.

HALPERN, JOEL M., 1958, *A Serbian Village*. New York: Columbia University Press.

HARING, D. G. (ed.), 1956, *Personal Character and Cultural Milieu*. 3d rev. ed. Syracuse, N.Y.: Syracuse University Press.

HARRIS, GEORGE L., 1958a, *Iraq*. New Haven, Conn.: Human Relations Area Files—Survey of World Cultures.

———, 1958b, *Jordan*. New Haven, Conn.: Human Relations Area Files—Survey of World Cultures.

HARRIS, MARVIN, 1956, *Town and Country in Brazil*. New York: Columbia University Press.

HENRIQUES, F. M., 1953, *Family and Color in Jamaica*. London: Eyre and Spottiswoode.

HENRY, JULES, 1963, *Culture against Man*. New York: Random House.

HERSKOVITS, MELVILLE J., 1948, *Man and His Works*. New York: Knopf.

HERSKOVITS, MELVILLE J., and FRANCES S. HERSKOVITS, 1933, *An Outline of Dahomean Religious Beliefs*. Memoirs of the American Anthropological Association No. 41. Menasha, Wisconsin: American Anthropological Association.

HILL, SHIRLEY, 1964, Cultural Differences in Mathematical Concept Learning. *American Anthropologist* Special Publication 66:201–222.

HITCHCOCK, JOHN, 1966, *The Magars of Banyan Hill*. New York: Holt, Rinehart and Winston, Inc.

HOBHOUSE, LEONARD T., G. C. WHEELER, and M. GINSBERG, 1915, *The Material Culture and Social Institutions of Simpler Peoples*. London: Chapman & Hall.

HOEBEL, E. ADAMSON, 1954, *The Law of Primitive Man*, Cambridge: Harvard University Press.

——, 1956, The Nature of Culture. In *Man, Culture, and Society*, Harry L. Shapiro (ed.). New York: Oxford, pp. 168–181.

——, 1958, *Man in the Primitive World*.

——, 1960, *The Cheyennes: Indians of the Great Plains*. New York: Holt, Rinehart and Winston, Inc.

——, 1967, Anthropological Perspectives on National Character. *Annals of the American Academy of Political and Social Science* 370:1–7.

HOGBIN, HERBERT IAN, 1934, *Law and Order in Polynesia*. New York: Harcourt.

HOMANS, GEORGE C., 1950, *The Human Group*. New York: Harcourt.

HOMANS, G. C., and D. M. SCHNEIDER, 1955, *Marriage, Authority and Final Causes*. New York: Free Press.

HONIGMANN, JOHN, 1949, *Culture and Ethos of Kaska Society*. New Haven: Yale University Publications in Anthropology No. 40.

——, 1954, *Culture and Personality*. New York: Harper & Row.

——, 1958, *Three Pakistan Villages*. Institute for Research in Social Science.

HOWARD, ALAN, 1966, Some Implications of Dominant Kinship Relationships in Fiji and Rotuma. Paper prepared for participation in Wenner-Gren Foundation for Anthropological Research Symposium on "Kinship and Culture," August 20–29. To be included in *Kinship and Culture*, in preparation, edited by Hsu.

HSU, FRANCIS L. K., 1943, The Myth of Chinese Family Size. *American Journal of Sociology* 48:555–562.

——, 1948, *Under the Ancestors' Shadow*. New York: Columbia University Press.

——, 1955, *Americans and Chinese: Two Ways of Life*. New York: Abelard-Schuman.

——, 1959, Structure, Function, Content and Process. *American Anthropologist* 61:790–805.

——, 1960, A Neglected Aspect of Witchcraft Studies. *Journal of American Folklore* 73, 287:35–38.

——, 1961a, American Core Value and National Character. In *Psychological Anthropology: Approaches to Culture and Personality*, Francis L. K. Hsu (ed.). Homewood, Ill.: The Dorsey Press, pp. 209–230.

——, 1961b, Kinship and Ways of Life. In *Psychological Anthropology: Approaches to Culture and Personality*, Francis L. K. Hsu (ed.). Homewood, Ill.: The Dorsey Press, pp. 400–456.

——, 1963, *Clan, Caste, and Club*. New York: Van Nostrand.

——, 1965, The Effect of Dominant Kinship Relationships on Kin and Non-kin Behavior: A Hypothesis. *American Anthropologist* 67:638–661.

——, 1966a, Dominant Kin Relationships and Dominant Ideas. *American Anthropologist* 68:997–1004.

——, 1966b, Kinship and Culture: New Considerations and Applications. Paper prepared for Wenner-Gren Foundation for Anthropological Research Symposium on "Kinship and Culture," August 20–29. To be included in *Kinship and Culture* in preparation, edited by Hsu.

——, 1966c, The United States and China. *Northwestern Review* 2:1:2–10.

———, 1967a, Christianity and the Anthropologist. *International Journal of Comparative Sociology* 8:1, 1–19.

———, 1967b, *Under the Ancestors' Shadow*. Rev. ed. New York: Natural History Press.

———, 1968a, Chinese Kinship and Chinese Behavior. In *China's Heritage and the Communist Political System*, Ping-ti Ho and Tang Tsou (eds.). Chicago: University of Chicago Press.

———, 1968b. Iemoto. A new chapter for the Japanese translation of *Clan, Caste and Club*, 1963. Tokyo: Baifukan.

———, 1968c, *Passage to Difference: Americans and Chinese*. Revision of *Americans and Chinese: Two Ways of Life*. New York: Natural History Press.

HSU, FRANCIS L. K., BLANCHE G. WATROUS, and EDITH M. LORD, 1961, Culture Pattern and Adolescent Behavior. *International Journal of Social Psychiatry* 7, 1:33–53.

HU SHIH, 1953, Ch'an (Zen) Buddhism in China: Its History and Method. *Philosophy East and West* 3, 1:3–24.

HUNT, ROBERT C., 1965, An Intellectual History of National Character Studies by British and American Anthropologists. Unpublished Ph.D. dissertation, Northwestern University.

HUTCHINSON, B., 1954, *Old People in a Modern Australian Community*. Victoria: Melbourne University Press.

HUTCHINSON, HARRY WILLIAM, 1957, *Village and Plantation Life in Northeastern Brazil*. Seattle: University of Washington Press.

HYMES, DELL, 1964, *Language in Culture and Society*. A Reader in Linguistics and Anthropology. New York: Harper & Row.

INKELES, ALEX, 1960, Industrial Man: The Relation of Status to Experience, Perception and Value. *American Journal of Sociology* 66:1–31.

INKELES, ALEX, and RAYMOND A. BAUER, assisted by David Gleicher and Irving Rosow, 1959, *The Soviet Citizen: Daily Life in a Totalitarian Society*. Cambridge, Mass.: Harvard University Press.

INKELES, ALEX, and DANIEL J. LEVINSON, 1968, National Character: The Study of Modal Personality and Sociocultural Systems. In *Handbook of Social Psychology*, Gardner Lindzey (ed.). Rev. ed. Reading, Mass.: Addison-Wesley, 1954.

IWAI, TAKAHITO, 1932, *The Outline of Tenrikyo*. Tambaichi, Japan: Tenrikyo Doyu-sha.

JOHNSON, CHARLES S., 1941, Growing up in the Black Belt. Washington, D.C.: American Council on Education.

KAPLAN, BERT, 1954, *A Study of Rorschach Responses in Four Cultures*. Papers of the Peabody Museum of American Archaeology and Ethnology, Vol. 42, No. 2.

———, 1961, Cross-Cultural Use of Projective Techniques. In *Psychological Anthropology*, Francis L. K. Hsu (ed.). Homewood, Ill.: The Dorsey Press, pp. 235–254.

KARDINER, ABRAM, and RALPH LINTON, 1939, *The Individual and His Society*. New York: Columbia University Press.

KARDINER, ABRAM, RALPH LINTON, CORA DuBois, and JAMES WEST, 1945, *The Psychological Frontiers of Society*. New York: Columbia University Press.

KARDINER, ABRAM, and LIONEL OVESEY, 1951, *The Mark of Oppression: a Psychological Study of the American Negro*. New York: Norton.

KARVE, IRAWATI, 1961, *Hindu Society—An Interpretation*. Poona: Deccan College.

KAUFMAN, HOWARD KEVA, 1960, *Bangkhuad: A Community Study in Thailand*. Association for Asian Studies Monographs, Vol. 10. Locust Valley, N.Y.: J. J. Augustin.

KEESING, FELIX M., 1958, *Cultural Anthropology*. New York: Holt, Rinehart and Winston, Inc.

KEUR, JOHN Y., and DOROTHY L. KEUR, 1955, *The Deeply Rooted: A Study of a Drents Community in the Netherlands*. New York: American Ethnological Society Monograph 25.

KINSEY, ALFRED C., W. B. POMEROY, and C. E. MARTIN, 1948, *Sexual Behavior in the Human Male*. Philadelphia: Saunders.

———, 1953, *Sexual Behavior in the Human Female*. Philadelphia: Saunders.

KITTREDGE, GEORGE LYMAN, 1929, *Witchcraft in Old and New England*. Cambridge, Mass.: Harvard University Press.

KLASS, MORTON, 1961, *East Indians in Trinidad—A Study of Cultural Persistence*. New York: Columbia University Press.

KLUCKHOHN, CLYDE, 1944, *Navaho Witchcraft*, Peabody Museum Papers, Vol. 22, No. 2. Cambridge, Mass.

———, 1958, The Evolution of Contemporary American Values. *Daedalus* Spring 1958:78–109.

———, 1962, Universal Categories of Culture. In *Anthropology Today: Selections*, Sol Tax (ed.). pp. 304–320. Chicago and London: The University of Chicago Press.

KLUCKHOHN, CLYDE, and W. H. KELLY, 1945, The Concept of Culture. In *The Science of Man in the World Crisis*, Ralph Linton (ed.). New York: Columbia University Press.

KOLARS, JOHN F., 1963, *Tradition, Season, and Change in a Turkish Village*. Department of Geography, Research Paper No. 82. Chicago: University of Chicago Press.

KORNHAUSER, ARTHUR W., HAROLD L. SHEPPARD, and ALBERT J. MAYER, 1956, *When Labor Votes, A Study of Auto Workers*. New York: University Books.

KRIGE, J. D., 1947, The Social Function of Witchcraft. *Theorea: A Journal of Studies of the Arts Faculty*, Natal University College 1:8–21. Reprinted in *Reader in Comparative Religion*, William A. Lessa and Evon Z. Vogt (eds.). New York: Harper & Row, 1958.

KROEBER, ALFRED L., 1944, *Configurations of Cultural Growth*. Berkeley, Calif.: University of California Press.

———, 1948, *Anthropology*. Rev. ed. New York: Harcourt.

KULP, DANIEL, 1925, *Country Life in South China*. New York: Columbia University Press.

LEACH, E. R., 1961, *Pul Eliya, A Village in Ceylon*. Cambridge: Cambridge University Press.

LEIGHTON, ALEXANDER, 1945, *The Governing of Men*. Princeton, N.J.: Princeton University Press.

LEVINE, DONALD, 1965, *Wax and Gold: Tradition and Innovation in Ethiopian Culture*. Chicago: University of Chicago Press.

LEVINE, ROBERT A., 1962, Witchcraft and Co-Wife Proximity in Southwestern Kenya. *Ethnology* 1:1:39–45.

LEVI-STRAUSS, CLAUDE, 1956, The Family. In *Man, Culture, and Society*, Harry L. Shapiro (ed.). New York: Oxford, pp. 261–285.

LEVY, MARION J., JR., 1953, Contrasting Factors in the Modernization of China and Japan. *Economic Development and Cultural Change* 2:161–197.

LEWIS, OSCAR, 1951, *Life in a Mexican Village: Tepoztlán Restudied*. Urbana, Ill.: University of Illinois Press.

———, 1958, *Village Life in Northern India*. Urbana, Ill.: University of Illinois Press.

Life, July 7, 1967, p. 17.

LINTON, RALPH, 1945, Foreword to Kardiner *et al.*, *Psychological Frontiers of Society*. New York: Columbia University Press, pp. v–xiii.

———, 1951, The Concept of National Character. In *Personality and Political Crisis*, Alfred H. Stanton and S. E. Perry (eds.). New York: Free Press, pp. 133–150.

LIPSET, SEYMOUR MARTIN, 1963, *The First New Nation*, New York: Basic Books.

LODGE, OLIVE, 1941, *Peasant Life in Jugoslavia*. London: Seeley, Service & Co.

LOUNSBURY, FLOYD G., 1964, The Structural Analysis of Kinship Semantics. In *Proceedings of the Ninth International Congress of Linguists*, Horace G. Lunt (ed.). The Hague: Mouton and Co., pp. 1073–1093.

LOWIE, ROBERT H., 1945, *The German People: a Social Portrait to 1914*. New York: Farrar, Straus.

———, 1954. *Toward Understanding Germany*. Chicago: University of Chicago Press.

LYND, ROBERT, and HELEN LYND, 1929, *Middletown*. New York: Harcourt.

————, 1937, *Middletown in Transition*. New York: Harcourt.

MADARIAGA, SALVADOR DE, 1928, *Englishmen, Frenchmen, Spaniards: An Essay in Comparative Psychology*. London: Oxford.

MADSEN, WILLIAM, 1964, *The Mexican-Americans of South Texas*. New York: Holt, Rinehart and Winston, Inc.

MAKAL, MAHMUT, 1954, *A Village in Anatolia* Sir Wyndham Deedes (tr.). London: Vallentine, Mitchell & Co.

MANDELBAUM, DAVID G., 1956, Social Groupings. In *Man, Culture, and Society*, Harry L. Shapiro (ed.) New York: Oxford, pp. 286–309.

MARETZKI, THOMAS W., and HATSUMI MARETZKI, 1966, *Taira: An Okinawan Village*. Six Culture Series, Vol. 7. New York: Wiley.

MARRIOTT, McKIM, 1955, Little Communities in an Indigenous Civilization. In *Village India*, McKim Marriott (ed.). Chicago: University of Chicago Press, pp. 171–222.

MARRIS, PETER, 1958, *Widows and Their Families*. London: Routledge.

MATSUMOTO, YOSHIHARU SCOTT, 1960, *Contemporary Japan: The Individual and the Group*. Philadelphia: American Philosophical Society.

MAYER, ADRIAN C., 1960, *Caste and Kinship in Central India; A Village and Its Region*. Berkeley, Calif.: University of California Press.

McCLOSKEY, HERBERT, 1953, Conservatism and Personality. *American Political Science Review* 52:27–45.

McGRANAHAN, DONALD V., 1946, A Comparison of Social Attitudes among American and German Youth. *Journal of Abnormal and Social Psychology* 41:245–257.

MEAD, MARGARET, 1928, *Coming of Age in Samoa*. New York: Morrow.

————, 1949, *Male and Female*. New York: Morrow.

————, 1951, *Soviet Attitudes toward Authority*. New York: McGraw-Hill.

————, 1954, The Swaddling Hypothesis: Its Reception. *American Anthropologist* 56: 3:395–409.

————, 1962, National Character. In *Anthropology Today: Selections*, Sol Tax (ed.). Chicago: The University of Chicago Press.

————, 1965, *And Keep Your Powder Dry*. (First published 1942.) New York: Morrow.

MEAD, MARGARET (ed.), 1937, *Cooperation and Competition among Primitive Peoples*. New York: McGraw-Hill.

METZGER, DUANE, and GERALD E. WILLIAMS, 1963a, Tenejapa medicine I: The curer. *Southwest Journal of Anthropology* 19:216–234.

————, 1963b, A Formal Ethnographic Analysis of Tenejapa Ladino Weddings. *American Anthropologist* 65:1076–1101.

MIDDLETON, JOHN, and E. H. WINTER (eds.), 1963, *Witchcraft and Sorcery in East Africa*. London: Routledge.

MINTURN, LEIGH, and JOHN T. HITCHCOCK, 1966, *The Rajputs of Khalapur, India*. Six Culture Series, Vol. 3. New York: Wiley.

MORRIS, CHARLES W., 1956, *Varieties of Human Value*. Chicago: University of Chicago Press.

MUENSTERBERGER, WARNER, 1951, Orality and Dependence among the Chinese. *Psychoanalysis and the Social Sciences* Vol. 3.

————, 1955, On the Biopsychological Determinants of Social Life (in memoriam of Geza Roheim 1891–1953). In *Psychoanalysis and the Social Sciences*, Muensterberger and Axelrad (eds.). Vol, 4:7–28. New York: International Universities.

MUENSTERBERGER, WARNER, and SIDNEY AXELRAD (eds.), 1947–1958, *Psychoanalysis and the Social Sciences*. Superseded by *The Psychoanalytic Study of Society* Vol. 1, 1960. New York: International Universities.

MURDOCK, GEORGE P., 1945, Common Denominator of Cultures. In *The Science of Man in the World Crisis*, Ralph Linton (ed.). New York: Columbia University Press, pp. 123–142.

————, 1949, *Social Structure*. New York: Macmillan.

————, 1956, How Culture Changes. In *Man, Culture, and Society*. Harry L. Shapiro (ed.). New York: Oxford, pp. 330–344.

————, 1959, *Africa: Its People and Their Culture History*. New York: McGraw-Hill.

MURPHY, GARDNER (ed.), 1953, *In the Minds of Men*. New York: Basic Books.

MYRDAL, GUNNAR, 1962, *An American Dilemma*. New York: Harper & Row.

NADEL, S. F., 1935, Witchcraft and Anti-Witchcraft in Nupe Society. *Africa* 8, 4.

————, 1942, *A Black Byzantium*. London: Oxford.

————, 1952, Witchcraft in Four African Societies: An Essay in Comparison. *American Anthropologist* 54:18–29. Reprinted in *Cultures and Societies of Africa*, Simon Ottenberg and Phoebe Ottenberg (eds.). New York: Random House, 1960, pp. 407–420.

NAROLL, RAOUL, 1962, *Data Quality Control—A New Research Technique*. New York: Free Press.

————, 1965, Galton's Problem: the Logic of Cross-Cultural Analysis. *Social Research* 32, 4.

NASH, MANNING, 1965, *The Golden Road to Modernity: Village Life in Contemporary Burma*. New York: Wiley.

NIHON MINZOKU GAKU TAIKEI (Outline of Japanese Folklore) 1958–1962 13 vols., by various authors. Tokyo: Hei Bon Sha.

NORBECK, EDWARD, 1954, *Takashima: A Japanese Fishing Community*. Salt Lake City: Utah University Press.

————, 1959, *Pineapple Town: Hawaii*. Berkeley, Calif.: University of California Press.

NORBECK, EDWARD, and GEORGE DeVos, 1961, Japan. In *Psychological Anthropology*, Francis L. K. Hsu (ed.). Homewood, Ill.: The Dorsey Press, pp. 19–47.

NORTH, ROBERT C., 1952, *Kuomintang and Chinese Communist Elites*. Stanford, Calif.: Stanford University Press.

NURGE, ETHEL, 1965, *Life in a Leyte Village*. American Ethnological Society, Monograph No. 40. Seattle: University of Washington Press.

OPLER, MORRIS E., 1950, Village Life in North India. Reprinted from Patterns for Modern Living, Division 3, Cultural Patterns. Chicago: The Delphian Society.

————, 1959, The Place of Religion in a North Indian Village. *Southwestern Journal of Anthropology* 15, 3.

ORENSTEIN, HENRY, 1965, *Goan: Conflict and Cohesion in an Indian Village*. Princeton, N.J.: Princeton University Press.

OSGOOD, CHARLES, 1964, Semantic Differential Technique in the Comparative Study of Cultures. American Anthropologist Special Publication 66:171–200.

OSGOOD, CORNELIUS V., 1951, *The Koreans and Their Culture*. New York: Ronald.

————, 1953, *Village Life in Old China*. New York: Ronald.

PALMER, H. R., 1926, *History of the First Twelve Years of the Reign of Mai Irdis Alooma of Bornu (1571–1583): Translated from the Arabic with Introduction and Notes*. Lagos, Nigeria: Government Printer.

PARSONS, TALCOTT, 1942, Age and Sex in the Social Structure of the United States. *American Sociological Review* 7, 55:604–616.

————, 1943, The Kinship System of the Contemporary United States. *American Anthropologist*, 45:22–38.

PITT-RIVERS, G. H., 1927, *The Clash of Culture and the Contact of Races*. London: Routledge.

PITT-RIVERS, J. A., 1954, *The People of the Sierra*. London: Weidenfeld and Nicolson.

POWDERMAKER, HORTENSE, 1950, *Hollywood: the Dream Factory*. Boston: Little, Brown.

REDFIELD, ROBERT, 1930, *Tepotzlan, a Mexican Village*. Chicago: University of Chicago Press.

————, 1941, *The Folk Culture of the Yucatan*. Chicago: University of Chicago Press.

————, 1955, *Peasant Society and Culture*. Chicago: University of Chicago Press.

————, 1956, *The Little Community*. Chicago: University of Chicago Press.

REDFIELD, ROBERT, and MILTON SINGER, 1952, The Cultural Role of Cities. In *Economic Development and Cultural Change, III*. Chicago: University of Chicago Press.

REES, A. D., 1951, *Life in a Welsh Countryside*. Cardiff, Wales: University of Wales Press.

———, 1956, *Gosforth: The Sociology of an English Village*. New York: Free Press.

———, 1963, *A West Country Village, Ashworthy: Family, Kinship and Land*. London: Routledge.

REICHEL-DOLMOTOFF, GERARDO and ALICIA, 1961, *The People of Aritama*. Chicago: University of Chicago Press.

RIESMAN, DAVID, 1950, *The Lonely Crowd*. New Haven, Conn.: Yale University Press.

RIVERS, W. H. R., 1914, *The History of Melanesian Society*. Cambridge: Cambridge University Press.

ROBB, J. H., 1954, *The Working Class Anti-Semite*. London: Tavistock Publications.

RÓHEIM, GÉZA (ed.), 1951, *Psychoanalysis and the Social Sciences, Vol. 3*. Vols. 1–5, *Unconscious*. New York: International Universities.

———, 1950, *Psychoanalysis and Anthropology: Culture, Personality and the 1947–1958*. New York: International Universities.

ROMNEY, A. KIMBALL, and ROY GOODWIN D'ANDRADE (eds.), 1964, Transcultural Studies in Cognition. *American Anthropologist* Special Publication Part 2, Vol. 66, No. 3. Report of a conference sponsored by Social Science Research Council Committee on Intellective Processes Research.

RYAN, BRYCE, 1953, *Caste in Modern Ceylon: The Sinhalese System in Transition*. New Brunswick, N.J.: Rutgers University Press.

RYAN, BRYCE, L. D. JAYASENA, and D. C. R. WICKREMESINGHE, 1958, *Sinhalese Village*, Coral Gables, Fla.: University of Miami Press.

SAHLINS, MARSHALL D., 1960, *Evolution and Culture*, with E. R. Service, Ann Arbor, Mich.: University of Michigan Press.

SAINSBURY, P., 1955, *Suicide in London*. London: Chapman & Hall.

SALIM, S. M., 1962, *Marsh Dwellers of the Euphrates Delta*. London School of Economics Monographs on Social Anthropology, No. 23. London: University of London.

SANDERS, IRWIN T., 1949, *Balkan Village*. Lexington, Ky.: University of Kentucky Press.

———, 1962, *Rainbow in the Rock: The People of Rural Greece*. Cambridge, Mass.: Harvard University Press.

SAPIR, EDWARD, 1924, Culture, Genuine and Spurious. *American Journal of Sociology* 29:401–491.

———, 1927, Anthropology and Sociology. In *The Social Sciences and Their Interrelations*, W. F. Ogburn and H. Goldenweiser (eds.). Boston: Houghton Mifflin.

SARGAISON, E. M., 1954, *Growing Old in Common Lodgings*. London: The Nuffield Provincial Hospitals Trust.

SCHAFFNER, BERTRAM, 1948, *Father Land*. New York: Columbia University Press.

SCHNEIDER, DAVID M., 1956, Review of *Psychoanalysis and the Social Sciences*, Warner Muensterberger and Sidney Axelrad (eds.), New York: International Universities Press; 1955, *American Anthropologist* 58:953–954.

———, 1961, Introduction: The Distinctive Features of Matrilineal Descent Groups. In *Matrilineal Kinship*, David M. Schneider and Kathleen Gough (eds.). Berkeley and Los Angeles: University of California Press.

———, 1968, *American Kinship: A Cultural Account*. Englewood Cliffs, N.J.: Prentice-Hall.

SCHNEIDER, DAVID M., and GEORGE C. HOMANS, 1955, Kinship Terminology and the American Kinship System. *American Anthropologist* 57:1194–1208.

SERVICE, ELMAN R., and HELEN S. SERVICE, 1954, *Tobatí: Paraguayan Town*. Chicago: University of Chicago Press.

SIMPSON, GEORGE EATON, 1940, The Vadun Service in Northern Haiti. *American Anthropologist* 42:236–254.

SINCLAIR, R., 1950, *East London*. London: Robert Hale.

SKINNER, G. WILLIAM, 1964–1965, Marketing and Social Structure in Rural China. *Journal of Asian Studies* 24: 3–44, 195–228, 363–400.

SMITH, ROBERT, and JOHN CORNELL, 1958, *Two Japanese Villages*. Ann Arbor, Mich.: University of Michigan Press.

SMITH, ROBERT J., and EUDALDO P. REYES, 1957, Community Interrelations with the Outside World: The Case of a Japanese Agricultural Community. *American Anthropologist* 59:463–472.

SOFUE, TAKAO, 1960, Japanese Studies by American Anthropologists. *American Anthropologist* 62:306–317.

SPINDLER, GEORGE D., 1948, American Character as Revealed by the Military. *Psychiatry* 11:3:275–281.

———, 1955, Education in a Transforming American Culture. *The Harvard Educational Review* 25:3:145–156.

SPIRO, MELFORD E., 1958, *Children of the Kibbutz*. Cambridge: Harvard University Press.

SRINIVAS, M. N., 1952, *Religion and Society Among the Coorgs of South India*. London: Oxford.

———, 1955–1956, A Note on Sanskritization and Westernization. *The Far Eastern Quarterly* 15:492–496. Reprinted In *Class, Status and Power*, Reinhard Bendix and S. M. Lipset (eds.). New York: Free Press, pp. 552–560.

STEWARD, JULIAN, et al., 1956, *The People of Puerto Rico: A Study in Social Anthropology*. Urbana, Ill.: University of Illinois Press.

STIRLING, PAUL, 1965, *Turkish Village*. London: Weidenfeld & Nicolson.

STOETZEL, JEAN, 1955, *Without the Chrysanthemum and the Sword*. New York: Columbia University Press (for UNESCO).

STOODLEY, BARTLETT H., 1957, Normative Attitudes of Filipino Youth Compared with German and American Youth. *American Sociological Review* 22:553–561.

SUMMERS, MONTAGUE, 1956, *Geography of Witchcraft*. University Books (London, 1927).

SUTHERLAND, ROBERT LEE, 1942, *Color, Class and Personality*. Prepared for the American Youth Commission. Washington, D.C., American Council on Education.

TAX, SOL, 1953, *Penny Capitalism*. Washington, D.C.: U.S. Government Printing Office.

TOWNSEND, PETER, 1963, *The Family Life of Old People*. Pelican ed. (First published 1957.) Baltimore: Penguin Books, Ltd.

TUMIN, MELVIN, 1952, *Caste in a Peasant Society*. Princeton, N.J.: Princeton University Press.

TURNEY-HIGH, H. H. 1953, *Chateau-Gérard: The Life and Times of a Walloon Village*. Columbia, S.C.: University of South Carolina Press.

WAGLEY, CHARLES, 1941, *Economics of the Guatemalan Village*. Memoirs of the AAA, No. 58.

WALLACE, ANTHONY, F. C., 1961, *Culture and Personality*. New York: Random House.

———, 1966a, Handsome Lake and the Decline of the Iroquois Matriarchate. Paper prepared for the Wenner-Gren Foundation for Anthropological Research Symposium on "Kinship and Culture," August 20–29. To be included in *Kinship and Culture* in preparation, edited by Hsu.

———, 1966b, *Religion: An Anthropological View*. New York: Random House.

WALLACE, ANTHONY F. C., and JOHN ATKINS, 1960, The Meaning of Kinship Terms. *American Anthropologist* 62:58–80.

WARNER, W. LLOYD, 1958, *A Black Civilization: A Study of an Australian Tribe*. New York: Harper & Row.

———, 1959, *The Living and the Dead* (Yankee City Series Vol. 5) New Haven, Conn.: Yale University Press.

WARNER, W. LLOYD, et al., 1949, *Democracy in Jonesville*. New York: Harper & Row.

WARNER, W. LLOYD, BUFORD H. JUNKER, and WALTER A. ADAMS, 1941, *Color and Human Nature*. Prepared for the American Youth Commission. Washington, D.C.: American Council on Education.

WARNER, W. LLOYD, and J. O. LOW, 1947, *The Social System of a Modern Factory.* Yankee City Series, Vol. 4. New Haven, Conn.: Yale University Press.

WARNER, W. LLOYD, and PAUL S. LUNT, 1941, *The Social Life of a Modern Community.* Yankee City Series, Vol. 1. New Haven, Conn.: Yale University Press.

————, 1942, *The Status System of a Modern Community.* Yankee City Series, Vol. 2. New Haven, Conn.: Yale University Press.

WARNER, W. LLOYD, and LEO SROLE, 1945, *The Social Systems of American Ethnic Groups.* Yankee City Series, Vol. 3. New Haven, Conn.: Yale University Press.

WARREN, RICHARD L., 1967, *Education in Rebhausen: A German Village.* New York: Holt, Rinehart and Winston, Inc.

WEBB, BEATRICE POTTER, 1926, *My Apprenticeship.* New York, London: Longmans.

WERNER, OSWALD, 1965, Semantics of Navaho Medical Terms. *International Journal of American Linguistics,* 31, 1.

————, in press, *Taxonomy and Paradigm: Two Semantic Structures.*

WEST, JAMES, 1945, *Plainville, U.S.A.* New York: Columbia University Press.

WHITE, HARRISON C., 1963, *An Anatomy of Kinship* (Mathematical Models for Structures of Cumulated Roles). Englewood Cliffs, N.J.: Prentice-Hall.

WHITE, LESLIE A., 1959, *The Evolution of Culture.* New York: McGraw-Hill.

WHITING, BEATRICE B. (ed.), 1963, *Six Cultures.* New York: Wiley.

WHITING, JOHN, 1961, Socialization Process and Personality. In *Psychological Anthropology,* Francis L. K. Hsu (ed.). Homewood, Ill.: The Dorsey Press.

WHITING, JOHN, and I. CHILD, 1953, *Child Training and Personality.* New Haven, Conn.: Yale University Press.

WHITING, JOHN, RICHARD KLUCKHOHN, and ALBERT S. ANTHONY, 1958, The Function of Male Initiation Ceremonies at Puberty. In *Readings in Social Psychology,* Eleanor E. Maccoby, F. Newcomb, and E. Hartley (eds.). New York: Holt, Rinehart and Winston, Inc.

WHITTEN, NORMAN E., JR., 1965, *Class, Kinship and Power in an Ecuadorian Town: The Negroes of San Lorenzo.* Stanford, Calif.: Stanford University Press.

WILBUR, GEORGE B., and WARNER MUENSTERBERGER (eds.), 1951, *Psychoanalysis and Culture: Essays in Honor of Géza Róheim.* New York: International Universities.

WILLIAMS, W. M., 1956, *The Sociology of an English Village: Gosforth.* London: Routledge; New York: Free Press.

WOLF, ERIC, R., 1966, Kinship, Friendship and Patron-client Relations in Complex Societies. In *The Social Anthropology of Complex Societies,* Michael Banton (ed.). New York: Praeger.

WOLF, MARGERY, 1968, *The House of Lim: A Study of a Chinese Farm Family.* New York: Appleton.

WOLFE, ALVIN W., 1954, The Institution of Demba among the Ngonje Ngombe. *Zaire* (*Belgian Congo Review*), 8:853–856.

WOLFENSTEIN, MARTHA and NATHAN LEITES, 1950, *The Movies: A Psychological Study.* New York: Free Press.

WYLIE, LAURENCE, 1957, *Village in the Vaucluse.* Cambridge, Mass.: Harvard University Press.

YANG, C. K., 1961, *Religion in Chinese Society.* Berkeley, Calif.: University of California Press.

YANG, MARTIN C., 1945, *A Chinese Village.* New York: Columbia University Press.

YOUNG, FRANK W., 1965, *Initiation Ceremonies, A Cross-Culture Study of Status Dramatization.* Indianapolis: Bobbs-Merrill.

YOUNG, MICHAEL, and PETER WILLMOTT, 1959, *Family and Kinship in East London.* 2d impression. London: Routledge.

————, 1960, *Family and Class in a London Suburb.* London: Routledge.

ZBOROWSKI, MARK, and ELIZABETH HERZOG, 1952, *Life is with People: the Jewish Little-Town in Eastern Europe.* New York: International Universities.

Village and Community Studies by Region

The beginning student searching for anthropological studies by region will find the following list a useful aid. This list is not, however, exhaustive, and is restricted to works in English. The reader is urged to develop his own more exhaustive regional bibliography.

Europe

Anderson and Anderson, *Bus Stop for Paris: The Transformation of a French Village* (1965)

Anderson and Gallatin, *The Vanishing Village: A Danish Maritime Community* (1964)

Banfield, *The Moral Basis of a Backward Society* (1958) (community in central Italy)

Barnett, *Poland* (1958)

Barth, *The Role of the Entrepreneur in Social Change in Northern Norway* (1963)

Bauer, Inkeles, and Kluckhohn, *How the Soviet System Works: Cultural, Psychological and Social Themes* (1956)

Blum and Blum, *Health and Healing in Greece: A Study of Three Communities* (1965)

Campbell, *Honor, Family and Patronage: A Study of Institutions and Moral Values in a Greek Mountain Community* (1964)

Dunn and Dunn, *The Peasants of Central Russia* (1967)

Friedl, *Vasilika: A Village in Modern Greece* (1962)

Friedmann, *The Hoe and the Book: An Italian Experiment in Community Development* (1960)

Halpern, *A Serbian Village* (1958)

Keur and Keur, *The Deeply Rooted: A Study of a Drents Community in the Netherlands* (1955)

Lodge, *Peasant Life in Jugoslavia* (1941)

Pitt-Rivers, *The People of the Sierra* (1954) (Spain)

Sanders, *Balkan Village* (1949)

Sanders, *Rainbow in the Rock: The People of Rural Greece* (1962)

Turney-High, *Chateau-Gérard: The Life and Times of a Walloon Village* (1953)

Warren, *Education in Rebhausen: A German Village* (1967)

Wylie, *Village in the Vaucluse* (1957) (French)

Zborowski and Herzog, *Life is with People: The Jewish Little-town in Eastern Europe* (1952) (This is not a study of a particular community, but provides us with a composite picture from many areas.)

The British Isles

Arensberg, *The Irish Countryman* (1937)

Arensberg and Kimball, *Family and Community in Ireland* (1948)

Dennis, Henriques, and Slaughter, *Coal is Our Life* (1956) (Wales)

Frankenberg, *Village on the Border: A Social Study of Religion, Politics and Football in a North Wales Community* (1957)

Geddes, *The Isle of Lewis and Harris; A Study in British Community* (1954)

Rees, *Life in a Welsh Countryside* (1951)

Rees, *Gosforth: The Sociology of an English Village* (1956)

Rees, *A West Country Village, Ashworthy: Family, Kinship and Land* (1963)

Sinclair, *East London* (1950)

Williams, *The Sociology of an English Village* (1956)

The Middle East

Ammar, *Growing up in an Egyptian Village* (1954)

Aryout, *The Egyptian Peasant* (1963)

Fuller, *Burauij: Portrait of a Lebanese Muslim Village* (1961)

Gulick, *Social Structure and Culture Change in a Lebanese Village* (1955)

Harris, *Iraq* (1958a)

Harris, *Jordan* (1958b)

Kolars, *Tradition, Season, and Change in a Turkish Village* (1963)

Makal, *A Village in Anatolia* (1954)

Salim, *Marsh Dwellers of the Euphrates Delta* (1962) (Iraq)

Spiro, *Children of the Kibbutz* (1958) (Israel)

Stirling, *Turkish Village* (1965)

India

Bailey, *Caste and the Economic Frontier: A Village in Highland Orissa* (1957)

Beals, *Gopalpur: A South Indian Village* (1962)

Berreman, *Hindus of the Himalayas* (1963)

Dube, *Indian Village* (1955)

Hitchcock: *The Magars of Banyan Hill* (1966)

Lewis, *Village Life in Northern India* (1958)

Mayer, *Caste and Kinship in Central India: A Village and Its Region* (1960)

Minturn and Hitchcock, *The Rajputs of Khalapur, India* (1966)

Orenstein, *Goan: Conflict and Cohesion in an Indian Village* (1965)

Srinivas, *Religion and Society among the Coorgs of South India* (1952)

Ceylon

Leach, *Pul Eliya: A Village in Ceylon* (1961)

Ryan, *Caste in Modern Ceylon: the Sinhalese System on Transition* (1953)

Ryan, Jayasena, and Wichremesinghe, *Sinhalese Village* (1958)

Ethiopia

LeVine, *Wax and Gold: Tradition and Innovation in Ethiopian Culture* (1965)

Pakistan

    Eglar, *A Punjab Village in Pakistan* (1960)
    Honigmann, *Three Pakistan Villages* (1958)

China

    Crook and Crook, *The First Years of Yangyi Commune* (1966)
    Fei, *Peasant Life in China: A Field Study of Country Life in the Yangtze Valley* (1939)
    Fei and Chang, *Earthbound China* (1945)
    Fried, *Fabric of Chinese Society* (1953)
    Gallin, *Hsin Ksing, Taiwan: A Chinese Village in Change* (1966)
    Gamble, *Ting Hsien, A North China Rural Community* (1954)
    Gamble, *North China Villages: Social, Political and Economic Activities before 1933* (1963)
    Hsu, *Under the Ancestor's Shadow* (1948 and 1967)
    Kulp, *Country Life in South China* (1925)
    Osgood, *Village Life in Old China* (1953)
    Skinner, *Marketing and Social Structure in Rural China* (1964–1965)
    Yang, *A Chinese Village* (1945)

Japan

    Beardsley, Hall and Ward, *Village Japan* (1959)
    Dore, *City Life in Japan* (1958)
    Embree, *Suye Mura: A Japanese Village* (1939)
    Maretzki and Maretzki, *Taira: An Okinawan Village* (1966)
    Norbeck, *Takashima, A Japanese Fishing Village* (1954)
    Smith and Cornell, *Two Japanese Villages* (1958)

Korea

    Osgood, *The Koreans and Their Culture* (1951)

Southeast Asia

    Kaufman, *Bangkhuad: A Community Study in Thailand* (1960)
    Nash, *The Golden Road to Modernity: Village Life in Contemporary Burma* (1965)
    Nurge, *Life in a Leyte Village* (1965) (Philippines)
    Fraser, *Fishermen of South Thailand: The Malay Villagers* (1966)

Latin America

    Adams, *A Community in the Andes: Problems and Progress in Muquiyauyo* (1959)
    Foster, *Empire's Children: The People of Tzintzuntzan* (1948)
    Foster, *Tzintzuntzan: Mexican Peasants in a Changing World* (1967)
    Gillin, *The Culture of Security in San Carlos* (1951) (Guatemala)
    Harris, *Town and Country in Brazil* (1956)

Hutchinson, *Village and Plantation Life in Northeastern Brazil* (1957)

Klass, *East Indians in Trinidad: A Study of Cultural Persistence* (1961)

Lewis, *Life in Mexican Village* (1951)

Madsen, *The Mexican-Americans of South Texas* (1964).

Redfield, *Tepotzlan, A Mexican Village* (1930)

Redfield, *The Folk Culture of Yucatan* (1941)

Reichel-Dolmotoff and Reichel-Dolmotoff, *The People of Aritama* (1961) (Colombia)

Service and Service, *Tobati: Paraguayan Town* (1954)

Steward and colleagues, *The People of Puerto Rico: A Study in Social Anthropology* (1956)

Tax, *Penny Capitalism* (1953) (Guatemala)

Tumin, *Caste in a Peasant Society* (1952) (Guatemala)

Wagley, *Economics of the Guatemalan Village* (1941)

Whitten, *Class, Kinship and Power in an Ecuadorian Town: The Negroes of San Lorenzo* (1965)

Suggested Readings

Community Studies

AMMAR, HAMED, 1954, *Growing Up in an Egyptian Village*. London: Routledge.

Gives a general description of social organization and life in a rural village of upper Egypt. Ammar's main interest is the pattern of child-training and socialization. He contends that the system of social relations and economic activity of the community determines the kind of learning that takes place, and that the typical behavior patterns and "world view" of the *fellaheen* can be explained by the childhood experiences of these villagers.

ARENSBERG, CONRAD, and SOLON T. KIMBALL, 1940, *Family and Community in Ireland*. Cambridge: Harvard University Press.

One of the first studies to present a functional analysis of community life in a literate Western society. The authors stress the importance of the Irish family system and the pattern of local community ties in shaping attitudes and behavior in County Clare, a typical Irish rural community.

BEARDSLEY, RICHARD K., JOHN W. HALL, and ROBERT E. WARD, 1959, *Village Japan*. Chicago: University of Chicago Press.

The most thorough study of a Japanese rural community to date; an interdisciplinary research team spent four years recording all aspects of community life in the village of Niiki in southwestern Honshu, a village typical of thousands of wet-rice growing communities in Japan. It concludes that rural Japanese society is not static; Niiki has been able to accommodate the changes of modernization with little apparent social disruption.

DORE, R. P., 1958, *City Life in Japan*. Berkeley and Los Angeles: University of California Press.

Study of Japanese urban life based mainly on formal questionnaire interviews of a representative sample of 100 individuals from a single ward in Tokyo. Dore suggests that the outlook and mode of life of the urban Japanese is becoming much like that of their Western counterparts, causing problems of adjustment. Only limited generalizations can be made because the ward studied is somewhat atypical and because the research was carried out while Japan was still under military occupation rule.

LYND, ROBERT S., and HELEN M. LYND, 1929, *Middletown*. New York: Harcourt.

A classic anthropological study of a small midwestern city. The Lynds' analytical framework and use of historical materials has been adopted as a model for many subsequent studies of contemporary literate civilizations.

MAYER, ADRIAN C., 1960, *Caste and Kinship in Central India*. Berkeley and Los Angeles: University of California Press.

A thorough analysis of the pivotal position of the caste system in determining ritual, economic, political, and social relations in a large village in central India. Mayer makes no generalizations about Indian society, but contends that in the Malwa region kinship ties are the primary basis for ordering intracaste behavior and relationships between villages.

NASH, MANNING, 1965, *The Golden Road to Modernity: Village Life in Contemporary Burma*. New York: Wiley.

Generalizations about social change in Burma are made on the basis of "microstructural analysis" of two village communities, an irrigated rice-growing community and a mixed-crop community, which represent the two major ecological adaptations of the villagers of upper Burma. Nash found wide divergencies in goals and a lack of communication between the rural villagers and the national elite government.

WARNER, W. LLOYD, 1963, *Yankee City*. 1 vol. Abridged ed. New Haven: Yale University Press.

An excellent introduction to the most thorough study of social class and social structure in an American community. This abridged volume contains excerpts of material originally presented in the five volume Yankee City Series.

WHITING, BEATRICE B. (ed.), 1963, *Six Cultures: Studies of Child Rearing*. New York: Wiley.

Detailed descriptions of socialization and child-rearing practices in six contemporary cultures, each based on a recent field study of a single community. The six fieldwork teams began with the same sets of questions and hypotheses about child rearing, thus, their reports contain a large body of comparable data. No explicit comparisons or generalizations are offered by the editor.

Studies of Whole Cultures

BENEDICT, RUTH, 1946, *The Chrysanthemum and the Sword*. Boston: Houghton-Mifflin.

The best of the efforts to "study culture at a distance." Relying completely on "secondary sources," Benedict attempted to reconcile certain apparent contradictions in Japanese behavior during World War II. The result is the most comprehensive synthesis of Japanese values, culture, and behavior published to date.

DEVOS, GEORGE, and HIROSHI WAGATSUMA (eds.), 1966, *Japan's Invisible Race: Caste in Culture and Personality*. Berkeley and Los Angeles: University of California Press.

An interdisciplinary study of the *Eta* outcastes of Japan, including both historical data and case studies of several rural and urban outcaste communities. Part Two offers a comparative sociology and psychology of caste, drawing on the Japanese data and studies of caste in Hindu India and elsewhere. Comparing the position of the *Eta* to that of the Negro in America, the authors conclude that racism and caste have the same psychological foundation: status anxiety.

HSU, FRANCIS L. K., 1955, *Americans and Chinese: Two Ways of Life*. New York: Abelard-Schuman.

A wide variety of data are analyzed to support generalizations about the ways of thinking and patterns of daily life in two complex literate societies. The author stresses the continuities in each system, and emphasizes basic differences in kinship organization to account for fundamental differences between the Chinese and American approaches to life. (Revised edition to be entitled *Americans and Chinese: Passage to Understanding*, New York: Natural History Press, 1969.)

INKELES, ALEX, and RAYMOND A. BAUER, 1959, *The Soviet Citizen*. Cambridge: Harvard University Press.

An analysis of the daily life, beliefs, values, desires, and frustrations of the Soviet citizen based on interviews and questionnaire responses of a large sample of Soviet exiles in western Europe and the United States. The authors find that totalitarianism is not incompatible with modern industrial society.

KARDINER, ABRAM, et al., 1945, *The Psychological Frontiers of Society*. New York: Columbia University Press.

Formulation of a psychoanalytic technique for studying the reciprocal relationship between personality and culture. Although much of this book deals with nonliterate cultures, the section on Plainville, U.S.A., illustrates the use of the concept of basic personality structure in analyzing a complex literate society.

KARDINER, ABRAM, and LIONEL OVESEY, 1951, 1952, *The Mark of Oppression: A Psychological Study of the American Negro*. New York: Norton.

Generalizations about Negro basic personality structure and Negro-white relations in America are based on 25 psychoanalytic case studies of urban Negroes. The data suggest that discrimination severely handicaps personality integration and forces psychological adaptive patterns that result in a distinct Negro personality type.

MEAD, MARGARET, and MARTHA WOLFENSTEIN (eds.), 1955, *Childhood in Contemporary Cultures*. Chicago: University of Chicago Press.

A collection of essays presenting a variety of techniques for studying child-rearing practices in literate civilizations. These range from psychological tests, interviewing techniques, and observation of play activities to the analysis of themes in films, children's literature, and child-training manuals, and are illustrated with data from French, German, American, Chinese, Soviet Russian, and east European Jewish cultures.

REDFIELD, ROBERT, 1941, *The Folk Culture of Yucatan*. Chicago: University of Chicago Press.

Classic concomitant variation study—comparing and contrasting the cultural patterns and social organization of a city, town, peasant village, and tribal village in Yucatan —which served as the empirical basis for Redfield's folk-urban continuum hypothesis, and for his analytical framework for describing the patterns of interaction between the cultural center of a complex literate society and the folk traditions at its periphery.

RIESMAN, DAVID, 1950, *The Lonely Crowd*. New Haven: Yale University Press.

Riesman contends that American national character has changed from that of the "inner-directed man," whose values and direction derived from the internalization of adult authority, to that of the "other-directed man," who draws his behavioral cues from his contemporaries and peers. He suggests causes for this change and considers its possible consequences for American culture.

ZBOROWSKI, MARK, and ELIZABETH HERZOG, 1952, *Life is with People: The Culture of the Shtetl*. New York: Schocken Books.

A unique re-creation of a defunct cultural system—the culture of the small eastern European Jewish community or *shtetl*. Using written documents and information from surviving informants, the authors capture the flavor of Jewish life in eastern Europe prior to World War II.

STUDIES IN ANTHROPOLOGICAL METHOD

GENERAL EDITORS

GEORGE AND LOUISE SPINDLER
Stanford University

UNDERSTANDING AN AFRICAN KINGDOM: BUNYORO
John Beattie, *Oxford University*

VISUAL ANTHROPOLOGY: PHOTOGRAPHY AS
A RESEARCH METHOD
John Collier, Jr., *San Francisco State College*

ANALYSIS OF PREHISTORIC ECONOMIC PATTERNS
Creighton Gabel, *Boston University*

HOW TO LEARN AN UNWRITTEN LANGUAGE
Sarah C. Gudschinsky, *Summer Institute of Linguistics*

THE STUDY OF LITERATE CIVILIZATIONS
Francis L. K. Hsu, *Northwestern University*

THE LIFE HISTORY IN ANTHROPOLOGICAL SCIENCE
L. L. Langness, *University of Washington*

MANUAL FOR KINSHIP ANALYSIS
Ernest L. Schusky, *Southern Illinois University*

BEYOND HISTORY: THE METHODS OF PREHISTORY
Bruce G. Trigger, *McGill University, Montreal*

FIELD METHODS IN THE STUDY OF CULTURE
Thomas Rhys Williams, *The Ohio State University*

Related Titles in
CASE STUDIES IN CULTURAL ANTHROPOLOGY

BUNYORO: AN AFRICAN KINGDOM
John Beattie

THE DUSUN: A NORTH BORNEO SOCIETY
Thomas Rhys Williams

HOLT, RINEHART AND WINSTON, INC.
383 Madison Avenue, New York 10017